Those Amazing

D0842087

Pg 168 : another stolen idea of "co-creation !
ie Lutute Amaun !!

→ Agar

pg 36³⁸ Pansubjectivism   pg 39 Epigenetics !
                                    Nobel !!
pg 52 Social Responsibility
              of SCIENCE ! → Nukes ete

SCIENCE AND *Soul*

Charles Birch, former Challis Professor of Biology at the University of Sydney, is one of the world's leading ecologists and winner of the Templeton Prize for Religion in 1990. His early investigations on insects led to an interest in popular ecology. He went on to study genetics and ecology at the University of Chicago and at Oxford, and helped lay the foundations for the new science of population biology. His search for a philosophy that could embrace both science and religion culminated in what he calls 'an ecological model of God'. He is 89 years old.

pg 107   → "Ameboid" have "feelings"
                             matter = mental

pg 9, 32, 87, 128, 130, 167-168, 186
      ↳ Whitehead - non-"emergent"

To Peter Farleigh
A loyal friend and constant inspiration in process thought.

SCIENCE

AND
Soul

CHARLES BIRCH

TEMPLETON FOUNDATION PRESS
PHILADELPHIA

Templeton Foundation Press
300 Conshohocken State Road, Suite 670
West Conshohocken, PA 19428
www.templetonpress.org

2008 Templeton Foundation Press Edition
First published in Australia by UNSW Press

Templeton Foundation Press helps intellectual leaders and others learn about science research on aspects of realities, invisible and intangible. Spiritual realities include unlimited love, accelerating creativity, worship, and the benefits of purpose in persons and in the cosmos.

Library of Congress Cataloging-in-Publication Data
Birch, Charles.
    Science and soul / Charles Birch. -- Templeton Foundation Press ed.
       p. cm.
    Includes bibliographical references and index.
    ISBN-13: 978-1-59947-126-6 (pbk. : alk. paper)
    ISBN-10: 1-59947-126-4 (pbk. : alk. paper) 1. Religion and science. I. Title.
    BL240.3.B57 2008
    215--dc22
                                    2007034097

Printed in Australia

08 09 10 11 12 13   10 9 8 7 6 5 4 3 2 1

CONTENTS

FOREWORD

To a casual observer the conflict between religion and science is both entrenched and unresolvable. Starting from the church's suppression of Galileo, religion has led a five centuries' long assault on truth, which has left the world in the shambles we are in. At least that is what the current anti-religion campaign, led by celebrity scientist Richard Dawkins, would have us believe.

The truth is quite different. The early empiricists were profound believers in God, and on account of their faith were propelled – like the great Swedish botanist, Carl Linnaeus to observe and catalogue the natural order with all its competitive species and remarkable adaptations. Linnaeus, like so many early scientists, including the medical researcher and mystic, Paracelsus, and the intrepid metaphysician-cum-cosmologist and ex-monk, Giordano Bruno, believed that the world they studied inhered in God and was continuous with His creative will. To them were afforded brilliant intuitive insights about the nature of the world, such as its atomic structure and the infinity of the universe, of which we must stand in awe since their discernment of such subtle matters predated the advent of powerful microscopes and telescopes. Indeed, Isaac Newton, who wrote more on the Bible than he did on science and also gave us the Law of Gravity, is yet another demonstration of the co-existence of belief in God and a keen scientific mind.

These examples of the productive relationship between the scientific and the spiritual quest have not been consigned to the fossil record of the history of ideas, like some ill-fated species, unable to produce offspring. In our own era, Albert Einstein, usually ranked as the 20th century's most important scientist, was not dissuaded of God's existence with his discovery of the special theory of relativity, but confirmed in it. So it is in that venerable tradition that Charles Birch, Australia's eminent ecologist and theologian, has urged a philosophical integration of spiritual and scientific ways of understanding life. It has not been a popular path to tread in an age when science and spirituality were generally considered irreconcilable opposites. With the help of some of the most eminent philosophers, theologians and scientists of the 20th century, this Melbourne-born biologist would develop a way of bringing these two 'opposites' together, and thereby climb the heights of what has become the holy mountain of the third millennium.

The idea that belief in God and a sophisticated understanding of the natural order, from evolutionary biology to the origins of the universe, should be possible and even integrated is a great intellectual challenge that faces the world. Not for Birch the quip by French biologist and Nobel Laureate Jacques Monod (1910–1976), that 'the scientist who believes in God suffers from schizophrenia'. Birch's entire body of work, from his early gem of a book, *Nature and God* (1965) to these late gleanings in the form of an intellectual memoir, demonstrates beyond a shadow of a doubt that Monod was wrong.

Of course, there are many ways to blend the scientific and the spiritual, and not all of them are recommended. We are currently seeing the popular notion of Intelligent Design, which posits a

God who not only created but fixed creation in its complexities of function and beauty. Many problems exist with that notion, including its fixity and the assumption that animals, flowers and human beings are designed for optimum functioning. It is a mechanical vision of nature and a belief in an interventionist God, which misses the depth of meaning that Birch discerns in existence. His meaning is born out of a relationship, in which God animates nature by persuasive love, elemental in all creation no matter how low it is on the evolutionary scale or how small its particles. By positing this relationship – of an interested God and a subjective nature (pansubjectivism) – Birch also makes a simple word or a feeling carry far more than we are used to giving it in formal treatises. Yet feelings are the sign of life, where emotion, intellect and the senses combine, and Birch is keen to place this at the centre of his philosophy, not least because it links us to the non-human world.

It is a long way from Charles' self-described fundamentalist Christian youth, with its fixed doctrines and literal reading of the Bible. One can only envy the journey that led him away from those early Evangelical Union days at the University of Melbourne and took him to the University of Chicago and Columbia University in the 1940s and 1950s where he was exposed to some of the greatest thinkers of the 20th century. They included Paul Tillich and Reinhold Niebuhr, lighting the path to liberal theology, and Charles Hartshorne whose mentor was Alfred North Whitehead, providing the entrée to process thought. Many more scholars, including evolutionary biologist Theodosius Dobzhansky and HG Andrewartha in Adelaide would become mentors and friends. The young Australian responded wholeheartedly to the challenges they posed a post-war world where both religious and scientific orthodoxies lay shattered and new paradigms were in the making. However, it would be process thought, which seeks to reconcile the diverse aspects of nature, and emphasises the developmental or becoming aspect of existence, that gave Birch the framework to reform his Christian faith into a theological and scientific synthesis. Others, such as theologian Harry Emerson Fosdick, the first minister of Riverside Church in New York, enabled Birch to think of Jesus as an affirmation of human nature, not as God: 'The God who was in Jesus … is the same God who is in us.'

Science, philosophy and theology can sound like hard work, and articulating an integrated worldview can lack an emotional appeal in academic writing. By contrast the Bible is richly served by the ardour and exuberance of the Psalms. This is where Charles' obvious love for poetry, especially the English Romantics, comes to the rescue. In so many of his books, his perfectly chosen poems stand as beacons, shining forth a vision that can make all the reasoned arguments seem but pale imitations. To them I return again and again, lingering over their artful encapsulation of the message of his work, like this fragment by the poet George Matheson:

> I give Thee back the life I owe,
> That in Thine ocean depths its flow
> May richer, fuller be.

With this memoir, the future of ecology, faith and philosophy will hopefully run to richer and fuller depths, knowing where some of their seminal ideas were born and matured, and were given full expression by Australia's unique scientist and theologian, Charles Birch.

Rachael Kohn

ACKNOWLEDGMENTS

I am grateful to Paul Ehrlich for his suggestion that became Chapters 1 to 4. Barbara Sanders provided all the help I needed to overcome computer problems that cropped up all along the way. For her help and guidance I am most grateful. I had the opportunity to discuss with John Cobb some key concepts in Chapters 5 and 6. This added greatly to clarity in my own mind and hopefully will be the case to the reader also. To John Cobb I owe a great debt of gratitude. David Paul, generous with his time and expertise, helped to compile the index.

INTRODUCTION

Build thee more stately mansions,
O my soul.

Oliver Wendell Holmes
'The Chambered Nautilus'

This book has a twofold origin. One of my professional colleagues suggested I should write about the people who influenced me as I knew them, not how others might have known them. Other colleagues suggested I should write a non-technical account of my view of life, known as process thought, as I understand it. I have tried to put these two proposals together. Indeed, one follows from the other as the people I have known contributed to my view of life. They are evolutionary biologists, ecologists, philosophers of religion and those concerned with science and religion.

My list of mentors does not include many important people in their areas because I did not know them well, or they did not greatly influence me. My emphasis is anecdotal and includes personal aspects and philosophical convictions. The living are, with some exceptions, not included except tangentially. For example, the discussion under the late Charles Hartshorne includes other process philosophers such as the contemporary John Cobb.

I try to be objective, but without the boldness of Alfred North Whitehead when he said of evolutionary biologist Thomas Henry Huxley:

He was just under the first rank, immensely able, but not as great as [Charles] Darwin. Darwin, on the other hand, is truly great but he is the dullest great man I can think of [Price 1954 p 283].

With fear and trembling

'Work out your salvation with fear and trembling' said St Paul (in Philippians 2:12). But it helps to have someone hold your trembling hand from time to time. And that applies not just to the weak but also to the strong. This is what Charles Darwin said about his time in college in Cambridge and in particular about his college friend Professor John Stevens Henslow:

> You have been the making of me from the first. I should never have cared much about natural history if it had not been for our friendship in Cambridge. And now much later on you have helped me make the most of the result of my voyage of discovery.

So it was with my mentors.

The answers are changing

William Sloane Coffin, when chaplain of Yale University, said that we can build a community out of seekers of truth but not out of possessors of truth. By possessors of truth he meant people who know it all and can learn from no one who has a different view of life and its meaning. It is my experience that those who have genuine convictions about the truth stay seekers all their lives. The truth may have been delivered once and for all to the saints. It is not delivered that way to us. Creeds may be good signposts. But they are bad hitching posts. They may be important starting points for an endless adventure.

A professor showed a visitor around his department. 'And how do you examine the students?' asked the visitor. 'That's easy' said the professor. 'We ask them the same questions each year.' 'But doesn't that make it too easy for the students?' 'No' said the professor. 'We change the answers.'

The answers are changing. For one thing the more we know the more there is to be known. Knowledge and understanding are not like a field with a fence around them. They are more like the surface of a balloon that is expanding all the time, with the surface coming into contact with an ever-widening area. In that endeavour Darwin said that 'looking back I think it was more difficult to see what the problems were than to solve them'. I think that is true of my mentors.

Science and religion are endlessly modifiable

Some people fear that science will eventually explain everything, that it will turn us and our knowledge into assemblages of molecules and sterile equations. After all physicists have talked about their quest for the 'theory that explains everything'. But they don't mean everything. They mean by everything the theory that will account for both relativity and quantum theory. That's not everything! An explanation of everything will never happen. This is because for every question answered a dozen new ones appear. And they are usually more challenging than the prior problems. Our present knowledge is but a drop in the ocean. Biologist TH Huxley said that life is not only stranger than we imagine, it is stranger than we can imagine.

Toward the end of his life Isaac Newton could still say:

I know not what the world may think of my labours, but to myself it seems I have been but as a child playing on the seashore; now finding some pebble rather more polished, and now some shell rather more agreeably variegated than another, while the immense ocean of truth extended itself unexplored before me [Anon 1954 p 761].

Science draws its strength from its cumulative nature in an infinite quest. In that quest later results modify earlier ones.

There is every reason why religion, like science, ought to be endlessly modifiable. But this is unlikely when religion claims that its truth comes via revelation. Truth is discovered by the mind so that every affirmation on any topic is subject to a critique as in science. Their validity and value change over time as is evident in the lives of many of my mentors such as Harry Emerson Fosdick. When people ask me if my views have changed over time I reply 'yes' and 'no'. Some foundational ideas stay, new ones are added, others change and yet others are cast aside. We should not throw away our tentative convictions leaving a vacuum before we have at least an inkling of what is to fill that vacuum. Otherwise the later state will be worse than the earlier.

Making explicable the inexplicable

There are some who draw a very narrow boundary to science, such as the proponents of so-called 'intelligent design'. Champions of this theory imply an 'intelligent designer' to be the cause of the order in nature. So what science has not yet explained, they claim, must be the result of a miracle such as a miraculous creation rather than the scientific understanding of evolution for the origin and evolution of life. This theory is the fruit of minds that regard that which has not yet been explained as inexplicable. In this view science has limited relevance. But the history of science is the history of that which was inexplicable becoming in time explicable. The order of nature or so-called design of nature was inexplicable in the 18th century. The dilemma was supposedly resolved by appealing to the supernatural and invoking a designer of nature, namely the deistic God. In the 19th century Darwin gave us a naturalistic explanation of creation in his theory of the origin of species. It involved three concepts: struggle for existence, variation and natural selection. They have been extensively investigated and, over time, developed in a way Darwin could hardly have foretold. No scientist could subscribe without qualification to Galileo's or Newton's beliefs or to his own beliefs of 10 years ago. But this is not a sign of defeat. Whitehead (1933b p 231) says that in the evolution of knowledge a contradiction can mark the first step in progress and this is one reason for tolerance of a variety of opinions. He reminds us that the duty of toleration is summed up in the biblical words 'Let both grow together until the harvest' (Matthew 13:30). Oliver Cromwell's cry echoes down the ages 'My brethren, by the bowels of Christ I beseech you, bethink you that you may be mistaken.'

Religion, said Whitehead, has to face change in the same way science does. 'Its principles may be eternal, but the expression of those principles requires continual development' (Whitehead 1933b p 234).

Whitehead said we may never fully understand but we can increase our penetration. After a lengthy discussion in committee on a difficult subject the first general secretary of the World Council of Churches remarked to a friend of mine that he was still confused but at a higher level! The role of reasoning in religion and science is to lead to understanding, not to proof. Our first understanding may well be in terms of a simple model. This was true of my own understanding of religion (as I describe). In my scientific field of population biology one approach is in terms of fairly simple mathematical models. This is valid so far as it goes, but it needs to be confronted with the complexity of nature which the field naturalist knows. In many cases nature is not simple at all.

While pursuing science as far as it goes it does not follow that science is the only source of knowledge. Science does not exhaust the content of things. It is not the only activity of the human spirit.

Knowledge shrinks as wisdom grows

In science and religion our first understanding is necessarily overtly simple. But we should not stay there if we are to have a mature understanding. We come to mistrust our simple understanding. Many, for example fundamentalists, stop there. 'Seek simplicity' said Whitehead 'and mistrust it.' The point is that mistrust can lead to a richer and more mature understanding that we were unable to appreciate in our earlier simple understanding. We convert the demise of one level of understanding into the birth of a successor. People worry about the impossibility of keeping pace with the huge increase in knowledge. But therein lies a fallacy. Knowledge shrinks as wisdom grows. This is because details are swallowed up in principles. The function of education is to shed details in favour of principles. In the process we may change our interpretation of what we are doing, though most scientists avoid this sort of philosophical analysis. By the sixth edition of *The Origin of Species* in 1876 Charles Darwin had convinced himself that he had been a good Baconian scientist, that is to say he thought he was immersing himself in a plethora of facts in nature that eventually spelled out a story. But his correspondence and autobiography tell a different story. He declared, for example, that he could not resist forming a hypothesis on every subject. He went into the jungle not with an empty head but with ideas hoping to find data to convince him one way or the other. Thought precedes imagination. Darwin had the germ of the idea of natural selection well before he had read Thomas Malthus, whose ideas on population were so influential in the formulation of Darwin's ideas on natural selection.

To fill up or draw out?

A university president once stated that his university was a reservoir of learning. Everybody brought some knowledge to it but no one took any away! The supply of knowledge is not like a service station from which one gets measured quantities of gas; it isn't about filling up. The root meaning of education is about drawing out. One of the most wonderful conversations between a teacher and a student is that between Plato and a slave named Meno in Plato's dialogue of that name. Plato doesn't tell him anything. He asks questions and draws the slave out. The slave finds the answers himself prompted by Plato. It is called non-directive counselling. Jesus did the same with the Samaritan woman by the well. He drew her out by asking questions about the well of water that could spring up forever in her life and so transform her. Education is like that. We ask questions about ourselves usually as a result of a challenge. Reinhold Niebuhr recognised two crises in knowledge which children face. One is when they find out that their parents are not as powerful as they thought. The second is when they find that their parents are not as good as they thought.

My purpose

I have published a number of books on different aspects of my worldview, which is known as process thought (see Birch in references), and which I explain later. None of these books covers the whole in synoptic form. The last two chapters in this book are not so much an account of what process thought is, but an account of what it means to me. Some things others may consider significant I have left out because they have not been important to me.

I am a biologist and so my scientific examples are mostly from biology, particularly evolutionary biology. Since the Renaissance two revolutions in biology have marked the birth of modern mechanistic biology. The first revolution came from René Descartes (*bête machine*) and William Harvey (the circulation of the blood). The second was Darwinism. Although *The Origin of Species* appeared in 1859 it was not until the 1940s that Darwinism really established itself in most branches of biology. These two revolutions are reflected in the thought of those who have influenced me. The organic philosophy of process thought was epitomised by AN Whitehead. It is a non-mechanistic, yet a fully scientific, understanding of nature.

Dogmatic fallacy

Profound as his views are Whitehead never regarded them as final statements or dogmas. 'There are no full truths' he said, 'all truths are half truths.' Furthermore Whitehead (1929 p xiv) reflected 'how shallow, puny, and imperfect are efforts to sound the depths in the nature of things. In philosophical discussion, the merest hint of dogmatic certainty as to the finality of statement is an exhibition of folly.' The dogmatic fallacy is 'the belief that the principles of its [the dogma's] working hypotheses are clear, obvious and irreformable' (Whitehead 1933a p 223). Dogmas may appear clear because they are simplistic, they may appear obvious because they exclude ramifications, and irreformable because they are regarded as unchanging truth.

The philosopher of science Charles Sanders Peirce said that the conclusions of science make no pretence to being more than probable. Degrees of certainty exist even there. In any particular case it may be difficult to put a figure on it. But at least we can recognise that 100 per cent certainty on complex issues is unlikely.

We make generalisations from experience. They are what Whitehead called 'adventures of ideas'. For some of us they have become the most exciting adventure of our lives. It is to boldly frame a system of ideas in terms of which *every* element of our experience can be interpreted. *Every* in this sentence covers the five senses of 'sensationalism' and non-sense experiences such as subjective valuation. That is the challenge. Degrees of uncertainty imply taking risks. Whitehead is aware of the risk in venturing into uncharted waters. It leads him to say 'It is the business of the future to be dangerous' (Whitehead 1933b p 259). It is better to take risks and fail than to take no risks at all.

Fallacy of misplaced concreteness ✓

The mechanistic theory of nature has reigned supreme since the 17th century. It is the model of nature as machinery. It was the orthodox creed of physics until the rise of quantum theory and is still the orthodox creed of biology. It has been highly successful in investigating those aspects of nature which are like machines, the heart as a pump and aspects of the brain like a computer. But it has been less successful as a guide to subjective aspects of nature such as feelings. To say that the heart or the atom is like machinery is a valid statement, but to say that they are machines is to commit what Whitehead (1933a p 64) called the fallacy of misplaced concreteness. It is to mistake the abstract for the concrete. Mechanism is an abstraction from nature. It is not concrete nature. Much of what I have to say of my view of life is a critique of materialism and a promotion of an organic view of nature. It is an attempt to give an appropriate place to subjective feelings. Cobb (1989 p 41) points out that avoiding misplaced concreteness is not easy. We cannot think without abstractions. To abstract literally means 'to draw away from'. We can draw away from concrete experience in different directions, but perhaps we shall never succeed completely.

Objectivity and subjectivity

When I look at a European forest in Spring I experience the colour green. In the Autumn I experience it as mostly the colour brown. These are two different experiences. In analysing these experiences the scientist gives us objective information. He might tell us that the experience of colour is associated with a particular area of the brain, that greenness is associated with electrical impulses in certain nerve cells in this area and that brownness is associated with electrical impulses in other cells. These are the biological correlates of the experience of colour. But there is also the subjective aspect of experience which is the feeling we ourselves have. There is a gap between the experience we have and what science has to tell us about it. Once you have the objective facts about an experience there are a lot of subjective facts left over such as my desires and my pains. The proposition here is that conscious experience is not simply reducible to what science as we know it has to tell us. Process thought is an attempt to bring the two together (as I hope to demonstrate).

'Nothing but' philosophies

We live at a time of 'nothing but' philosophies. Each of us is nothing but a pack of nerve cells, says the neurophysiologist. The human mind is nothing but a computer programme, says the exponent of artificial intelligence. We are nothing but lumbering robots whose genes create us body and soul, says the sociobiologist. My response to all these statements is: none of the above. I recall a Viennese joke about two neighbours. One of them contended that the other's cat had stolen and eaten two kilos of butter. There was a bitter argument and finally they agreed to seek the advice of a rabbi. They went to the rabbi and the owner of the cat said 'It cannot be my cat, it does not eat butter.' The other insisted the cat did it. 'Bring me the cat' said the rabbi. They brought the cat to him and the rabbi said 'Bring me the scales.' They brought the scales and the rabbi asked, 'How many kilos of butter?' 'Two kilos' said the complaining neighbour. Believe it or not the weight of the cat was exactly two kilos. So the rabbi said, 'Now I have the butter, but where is the cat?' We may well ask the 'nothing but' philosophers: 'But where is the human?' Whitehead finds something missing in Darwinism when he says 'Darwin and Huxley had grasped the principle of evolution but it never occurred to them to ask how evolution of materials could result in a man like, let us say, Newton' (Price 1954 p 283). Where in Darwinism is the human? Where is Newton? These are central questions for process thought which I discuss in some detail later.

It is obvious that my list of persons who influenced me reflects the meaning of life I have come to understand. I present my case with reference to the nature of contrary points of view without analysing these in detail. I have about 20 persons in my list of those I knew well and my account of them comes first. It is not primarily an account of their work but their thoughts and personality. My project grew from that beginning. I ask: 'What do all these influences add up to in my own thinking and ideas?' My answer is in Chapters 5 and 6.

On being interesting even if not true

Of my mentors it could be said that what they said and wrote was interesting. I doubt that I would have been drawn to them but for this. JBS Haldane urged his colleagues to produce something that was 'interesting, even if not true'. Whitehead (1929 p 259) in a similar vein said 'In the real world it is more important that a proposition be interesting than that it be true. The importance of truth is that it adds to interest.' He was not saying truth was unimportant. He was saying that the important thing was to be interesting and that would lead to truth.

I am compelled to add that what I have written are my convictions and in particular my understanding of process thought. It may be that some of my propositions are contradictory. Others may be judged as superficial, for I may say in one sentence what the expert puts in 20! My brevity may lead to greater clarity. At least that is my hope. In biology laboratory rats are trained to make their way through a maze to find their reward of food. I find myself in a maze in which some of the alleys are blind. But not all.

O world invisible, we view thee,
O world intangible, we touch thee,
O world unknowable, we know thee,
Inapprehensible, we clutch thee!

[**Francis Thompson**, 'The Kingdom of God']

1 EVOLUTIONARY BIOLOGISTS

Evolutionary biologists filled the missing links in Charles Darwin's theory of the mechanism of evolution. They are, for the most part, geneticists who had to do with the origin and inheritance of genetic variation. This was the major missing element in Darwin's theory. The reason is simple. When Darwin wrote *The Origin of Species* there was no substantial understanding of genetics. The combination of Darwinism and genetics became known as the evolutionary synthesis or neo-Darwinism. It was established in the first half of the 20th century. Its founders were Ronald Fisher and JBS Haldane in England, Sewall Wright and Theodosius Dobzhansky in the USA and SS Chetverikov in Russia. Five books published between 1937 and 1950 established evolutionary synthesis as the new foundation of evolutionary biology. In chronological order these books were: *Genetics and the Origin of Species*, by Theodosius Dobzhansky (1937); *Evolution: The modern synthesis*, by Julian Huxley (1942); *Systematics and the Origin of Species*, by Ernst Mayr (1942); *Tempo and Mode in Evolution*, by George Gaylord Simpson (1944) and *Variation and Evolution in Plants*, by Ledyard Stebbins (1950).

The genetic theory of Darwinian evolution heralded a revolution in biology that has continued to this day. It is comparable to the later one in molecular biology, when James Watson and Francis Crick in 1953 discovered the molecular structure of DNA.

I am not primarily a geneticist, so what had I to do with evolutionary biologists? The answer is that evolutionary biology has another side to it besides genetics, and that is ecology. If you read Chapter 3 of Darwin's *The Origin of Species* entitled 'Struggle for Existence' you will be reading a great work in ecology. I am an ecologist and that explains my involvement in evolution. Here is just one example. An insect called the Queensland fruit fly is native to Queensland. It lays its eggs into ripe fruit that is eaten by the larvae that hatch from the eggs. In the Australian tropics wild fruits grow in abundance, a veritable feast for the fruit fly. But south of the tropics few native soft fruits existed until humans planted fruit trees. The fruit fly spread thousands of kilometres to the southern states following the planting of fruit trees. It came to thrive in non-tropical climates. My colleagues and I were able to show that the fruit fly was able to spread because its genetic constitution changed to enable it to live beyond the tropics. This is an evolutionary change sometimes referred to as micro-evolution. The point is that the distribution and abundance of the Queensland fruit fly, its ecology, could be understood by studying not only its ecology but its evolutionary genetics also. So an ecologist needs to know something about evolutionary biology. That is how I became involved with the evolutionary biologists discussed in this section. My closest association was with the geneticists Theodosius Dobzhansky and Sewall Wright in the USA. I went to Columbia University in New York for a year and to Brazil for a year to work with Dobzhansky and he came to work with me in the University of Sydney for the best part of a year. I learned about genetics. He learned about ecology.

There are many distinguished evolutionary biologists, such as Ernst Mayr (ornithologist) and George Gaylord Simpson (palaeontologist), whose work is not discussed in this chapter. I knew them when both were at Columbia University but with a lesser involvement than I had with those discussed in this chapter. The purpose of this chapter is not to discuss evolutionary biology in detail, but some of the people behind it, their particular human characteristics and their philosophy of life, as I understood it. I was particularly interested as to whether they were materialists or not and how they reacted to my philosophy of life, which is non-materialistic.

Theodosius Dobzhansky

(Courtesy of Charles Birch)

Theodosius Dobzhansky (known to his colleagues as Doby or Dodick) was one of the founders of the evolutionary synthesis of Darwinism and genetics, sometimes known as neo-Darwinism, in the first half of the 20th century. Dobzhansky demonstrated the importance of genetic variation between individuals at the level of the gene and the chromosome. This has been the cumulative work of 50 years. 'What is remarkable about the development of this work' says Richard Lewontin 'is that a single central figure,

Theodosius Dobzhansky, planned and carried out the largest part of the experiments, and much of what has been done by others has been inspired by his work and ideas' (Lewontin 1981 p 94).

I first met Dobzhansky when I was on my way through New York to spend a year in the University of Chicago in 1946. I called upon him at Columbia University in New York where he was a professor of genetics. He pulled out from a drawer a recent paper by himself and Sewall Wright (of the University of Chicago) which clearly demonstrated Darwinian natural selection in nature. He had good evidence that the genetic constitution of populations of the fruit fly *Drosophila pseudoobscura* changed adaptively with the seasons and from place to place. It fitted well with the mathematical model of Sewall Wright. Pointing to the mathematics in the paper Dobzhansky said to me: 'that's Sewall Wright, the data from the field and from the lab is mine'.

So began a friendship with Dobzhansky which continued until his death in 1975. He was the age of the century. I still have the telegram telling me of his death (from leukaemia) from professor Ledyard Stebbins at the University of California in Davis 'Dobzhansky died suddenly 10.30 am December 18'. The *New York Times* ran a long obituary the next day. It commented on his book *Genetics and the Origin of Species* (1937) as 'one of the most important books of its kind since Charles Darwin's classic volume'. It has been described as a landmark work indicating a new stage in the problems of evolution in terms of modern cytogenetics. In his book Dobzhansky stated his profound belief that 'Nothing in biology makes sense except in the light of evolution.'

I worked with Dobzhansky at Columbia University in 1953 and in Brazil in 1955. Dobzhansky spent most of 1960 at the School of Biological Sciences, University of Sydney in joint projects. At the

University of Sao Paulo four of us, Dobzhansky, Bruno Battaglia of Padua, Ove Friedenberg of Copenhagen and myself were financed by an organisation called 'Organisation for the promotion of superior people in Brazil'! The superior people were not us but students. This project was also financed by the Rockefeller Foundation in New York. Besides our teaching, we had research projects, the main one being on tropical islands south of Rio at Angra dos Reis (Haven of Kings). The project was to use some of the islands as giant 'cages' for experiments on natural selection in fruit flies. It involved many enjoyable visits to this tropical haven. In the end it seemed that our islands were not as isolated as they needed to be for the purposes of our experiments, and the projects had to be abandoned. However, we did research on other topics that added to our knowledge of natural selection in nature.

In Sao Paulo I shared with Dobzhansky a room in a pension in Avenida Sao Paulo within walking distance of the laboratory. We had a strict routine each day. It included a brief siesta after a heavy mid-day meal. On the first Wednesday Dobzhansky disappeared for a while, returning in the late afternoon with a dozen cream cakes which he purchased downtown. I found some difficulty in consuming my half. When the next Wednesday came he said to me, now it is your turn to get the dozen cream cakes. What you ask for is 'un doze doces'. I duly found the cake shop but had difficulty with my Portuguese and eventually had to point to what I wanted. When I got back with my purchase Dobzhansky told me that I had said to the girl behind the counter: 'You sweet of sweets!' Well I wonder. For some weeks I kept up with this routine until six cream cakes became too much for me. I announced that I couldn't cope any more. 'You must be sick,' he said. But I stuck to my guns about the cakes.

Every Sunday night we would walk towards the city down Avenida Sao Paulo to a rather uninviting white-tiled restaurant where we always ordered Soupa de Palmeto; soup made from the heart of palms. These were happy interludes in between serious work and also what Dobzhansky found exasperating periods of Brazilian casualness. On one occasion all was teed up for going to Angra dos Reis when the Brazilian professor, Crodowaldo Pavan, decided to attend a wedding instead. Then there were political disruptions called sieges when banks, post offices and all government offices came to a standstill. Our lab happened to be a stone's throw from the palace of the governor of the state of Sao Paulo, Janio Quadros. He was at loggerheads with the mayor of the city and had issued instructions that all repairs of the city's buses cease. On this day we heard a commotion and there was the governor chasing the mayor out of the palace gates. So were political battles dealt with. Janio Quadros later became president of Brazil.

Cuiabá is the capital of the state of Mato Grosso. A stone column standing in the middle of the town claims it to be the geographic centre of South America. On our visit it was a sleepy town of 3000 inhabitants and also a refuge for escaped Nazis. When we asked a citizen leaning against a lamp post what he did he said 'I live here', which was an unexpected but good reply. Our objective was to collect fruit flies at the southern edge of the Amazon rainforest. To get there we needed the services of the secretary of a rubber collecting company that tapped native rubber trees in the region. His name was Prince Eugene Wittelsbach of the royal house of Bavaria and said to be an ex-professor of philosophy in Germany. In the process of trying to find the prince we sought the mayor, by knocking on many doors. Along the way we met a lad whose name was Hitler but since h's are silent in Portuguese he went under the name Itle. At the airport we were accosted by an American missionary who wanted to know if Dobzhansky was saved. Dobzhansky found this very embarrassing so I replied on his behalf. I remembered later that an appropriate reply would have been: 'I'm damned if I'm not.'

From the Cuiabá airstrip the prince flew us in a small aircraft for two hours north to the field headquarters of his rubber company on the southern edge of the Amazonian rainforest. Here was a small wooden shack which was a dormitory for the rubber workers. We had it to ourselves. Despite the heat the wooden shutters were locked at night and under each pillow was a pistol. Back in Cuiabá we had hammocks for the night. Dobzhansky identified on my hammock a Reduviidae bug responsible for the transmission of Chagas disease otherwise known as *Brazilian trypanosomiasis*. Charles Darwin had symptoms which some interpreted as Chagas disease acquired in South America. On 26 March 1835, when spending a night in a village in the Argentine province of Mendoza, Darwin was bitten by the blood-sucking bug that is vector of the micro-organism *Trypanosome cruzi*. He may have contracted the disease. He was sick for the last 40 years of his life. I don't think I was bitten by the offending bug.

Despite the rigours of fruit fly-hunting Dobzhansky showed incredible excitement and enthusiasm to be anywhere near a tropical rainforest that would have its special fruit flies waiting for him.

One of Dobzhansky's great enthusiasms was horse riding. An opportunity came high up in the Andes where Chile meets Argentina. He thought this was my chance too and pressed a horse upon me, even though I had never been riding before. So we set out to get a good view of Aconcagua, the highest mountain in the western world. My horse had its own ideas; one being to get as close as it could to the edge of a huge canyon. At intervals crosses indicated that someone had lost their life. My horse galloped on regardless of my attempts to control it. Dobzhansky rode stately ahead, greatly amused at my incompetence which he thought was unfitting for an Australian. I spent the next day in bed and never rode again.

After adventuring in the Andes Dobzhansky had to return to his missionary quest. He travelled to Punta Arenas (which claims to be the southernmost city in the world at 53 degrees south) where he gave lectures on genetics and thus 'preach[ed] the gospel of genetics to the uttermost ends of the Earth'.

Early on in my year at Columbia University Dick Lewontin (now a professor at Harvard University) 'the smartest man I have ever met' (wrote Stephen Jay Gould), was then a graduate student of Dobzhansky. He and I were having a lively conversation in my lab. Dobzhansky knocked on the door, entered and asked what we were discussing. Lewontin replied to his supervisor that he wouldn't understand for we were discussing philosophy! Dobzhansky didn't take kindly to this remark from a graduate student but came to me later to say he was interested and invited me to his home for a discussion. He was deeply spiritually attached to his native Russia, had strong bonds with the Russian Orthodox Church, though he was not a regular worshiper. He had imbibed much from Fyodor Dostoevsky, Nicholas Bergaev and Leo Tolstoy and more recently from Pierre Teilhard de Chardin. And so that evening began a discussion between us on philosophy and religion that lasted through the decades ahead.

I was at that time attending a course on Protestantism and Culture at Columbia University given by the eminent theologian Paul Tillich. I invited Dobzhansky to join me, which he did. He was very taken by the famous Tillich phrase 'ultimate concern' (see

Chapter 3). We have many concerns that are secondary. But some are ultimate in the sense of fulfilling life. This too is Tillich's meaning of God in human life. Instead of using the name 'God' he replaces it with the two words: 'ultimate concern'. The immediate issue for Dobzhansky was a biological one. Why should we have evolved such concern? He gave his answer in a book with the unusual title *The Biology of Ultimate Concern* (1967). There is not much Tillich in this book but it did give, for the first time, Dobzhansky's philosophy of religion. The final chapter 'The Teilhardian Synthesis' came as a shock to his colleagues, particularly to Professor Ernst Mayr and Professor GG Simpson, both stalwarts of a strictly mechanistic view of evolution. Teilhard was a Jesuit and palaeontologist and had a strong mystical component in his synthesis, which had become widely known through his book *The Phenomenon of Man* (1955). Geneticists blamed me for having led Dobzhansky astray. But that was not the case. Dobzhansky was taken by Teilhard's concept of evolution having an ultimate goal: the Omega point. On the other hand Dobzhansky rejected a central Teilhardian concept 'the inner aspect' of all entities. This concept is akin to a view known variously as panpsychism, process thought, panexperientialism and pansubjectivism (see Chapters 5 and 6). It has been advanced by eminent philosophers such as AN Whitehead and Charles Hartshorne as well as by distinguished biologists such as Sewall Wright, Bernhard Rensch, Alister Hardy and Conrad H Waddington. Being a supporter of this concept myself I have had many discussions with Dobzhansky on it. The critical issue is: 'Can mind evolve from no mind?' We come to that question again when we discuss Sewall Wright whose answer was 'no' while Dobzhansky's answer was 'yes'. The question reveals a philosophical divide between biologists and is pursued in later chapters.

Colleagues have asked me if Dobzhansky had traditional religious views. I know he sporadically attended a Russian Orthodox liturgy at the church of Saint Seraphin in New York. And he had an honorary doctorate in theology from the Russian Orthodox Seminary in New York. Unknown to most of his colleagues he spent at least a week at the monastery on Mount Athos in Greece in his latter years. He had a fairly orthodox view of the resurrection and other doctrines. The liturgy seemed to fill a lot of spaces. The one occasion of the liturgy which I experienced in Tambov in central Russia filled me with awe as I witnessed the eager response of peasants. It filled something missing in their lives, which Tolstoy wished he had too. I think it did that also for Dobzhansky, even though he only attended the liturgy rarely. He was extremely emotional about situations such as experiencing a rainforest in the tropics or being in a place for the last time. When we came upon the Christ of the Andes high in the mountains facing the Pacific Ocean I took a photo of Dobzhansky that could be called 'Dobzhansky of the Andes'. This was a spiritual moment. Religion for him was emotional rather than cognitive. Memory too could be a highly emotive experience. When I visited him three months before his death he envied me the years that were between us and which were gone for him. He desperately wanted not to die. Following publication of *The Biology of Ultimate Concern* he sent me copies of correspondence between himself and Ernest Nagel who was at that time professor of philosophy at the Rockefeller University in New York. After reading this book Nagel wrote to Dobzhansky:

My main difficulty is with the supposition that life in general, as distinct from individual living creatures who are capable of deliberation and choice, might have a 'meaning' – especially since I believe with you that no 'aim' or 'purpose' directs the course of either cosmic or biological evolution ... I fail to grasp why a man's life can be genuinely meaningful only if his efforts are believed to contribute to the realization of some inclusive global goal, or only if he is committed to the view that cosmic changes are in some sense 'progressive' ... human lives can be meaningful even though the lot of man is eventual oblivion.

Dobzhansky replied in no uncertain terms:

I must disagree with you if by 'human lives can be meaningful, even though the lot of man is eventual oblivion' you mean the lot of mankind rather than as a person. No, if mankind ends in oblivion, life becomes extinct, and the universe lifeless and 'spiritless', then I want no part in this 'devil's vaudeville'. This, of course, is the old Dostoevskian problem, and this is the heart of my 'religion', as it was the heart of Teilhard's religion ... This does not mean that there exists an 'aim' or 'purpose' directing evolution by sticking its little finger into the machinery at critical moments to make it work according to the 'aim'. I have tried to make clear the absence of 'God of the gaps'. Should we accordingly abandon the hope that the universe is some sort of an undertaking? The wish surely may be the father of hope. But this wish is the true Dostoevskian style (after all I am his remote relative), too strong in me to resist.

Dobzhansky accepted the probability that life would become extinct on Earth. He could not accept that this would be the end of all that might have been achieved in cosmic, biological and cultural evolution. He could not face life with the view that man gives himself meaning in a universe itself devoid of meaning and value. He was convinced that if we have no value for the cosmos, we have no value period. We return to this issue in Chapters 5 and 6.

Two things deeply influenced Dobzhansky's understanding of life. One was the war years of his youth in Russia. The other was his adventurous life as a naturalist beginning in the Caucasus and eventually extending from Alaska to Tierra del Fuego. He was born in the small city of Nemirov in the Ukraine in 1900. Great social and political unrest stirred Kiev during the last years of World War I and the beginning of the Bolshevik era. Fifteen changes of government rocked Kiev from 1917 to 1920. In May 1920 Dobzhansky and his mother were literally starving. Dobzhansky went in search of food and came home with a piece of stale bread. His mother choked on the morsel and died within minutes. Life was precarious for Dobzhansky until 1927 when Dobzhansky and his wife Natasha went to Columbia University in New York, with the help of the Rockefeller Foundation, to work with the famous geneticist TH Morgan. He never returned to Russia.

I remember Dobzhansky as the most electrically energetic scientist I have ever known. He was enthusiastic for science in season and out of season. That is revealed in the many students who wanted to study under him and who became infected with his enthusiasm. His greatest student was Richard Lewontin now professor at Harvard University.

In some places the image of the scientist as a cold and passion-less person is still propagated. Dobzhansky incarnated the opposite: a person of flesh and blood, of passion and drive, of daring and courage. He argued with great vigour. The decibels would rise to a great crescendo. I recall Dick Lewontin saying that when he eventually conceded that you may have one chance in a thousand of being right then you had won the argument. I never won the argument with him about the basic nature of the world whether it consists of bits of mere matter or whether its ultimate entities have a subjective or mental aspect to them. The latter is what I argue for. Teilhard de Chardin, whom Dobzhansky admired, spoke of 'the inner aspects of things', by which he referred to the subjective nature of entities such as electrons and molecules as well as human beings and other living creatures. Dobzhansky simply ignored this part of Teilhard's thesis. He seemed not to like entertaining this concept in his mind and would dismiss the subject in caricature. This puzzled me as I regard the issue of great importance in my philosophy of life as I try to show later. Perhaps it has taught me that great minds such as Dobzhansky and the evolutionary biologist Sewall Wright (see later) can look at the same world and reach quite different conclusions. But, of course, it is not the same world they look at. The emperor has no clothes.

Dobzhansky was no narrow specialist, but lectured and wrote very successfully for a wider public on social and ethical issues. His mind was razor sharp getting to the point while we lesser mortals were still struggling. We also remember him as a deeply affectionate friend.

It was partly Dobzhansky's friendship with Professor Michael Lerner of the department of genetics at the University of California, Berkeley, that I was invited to teach for a semester in Lerner's department in 1960. There was a second reason and that was Lerner's interest in ethical issues in genetics. Yet a third and probably the most important reason for the invitation at that time was that it was the height of student protest against the Vietnam War and was also the height of the hippie movement amongst students. Lerner was interested in all these issues and knew I would be also. My official responsibilities were to give an undergraduate course in evolution and a graduate seminar in population biology (evolution and ecology). My introduction to students was in a bookshop in Telegraph Avenue. I was looking at a book on the shelf and a student nearby turned to me with an open book and said: 'Look at this, it will blow your mind!' I just couldn't imagine that happening in Sydney. My undergraduate class turned up with balloons and flowers and their dogs. I was given an apple for the teacher. What impressed me most were the weekly protest meetings outside the main administration building. Those against the Vietnam War had formed a Committee on Conscience to support students who refused to be called up for war service. The committee consisted of students and staff. On my return to Sydney I immediately formed a Committee on Conscience there. It became known to students through mass lunch-hour meetings on the front lawn of the University of Sydney. We offered free legal advice and friendly help as well as visits to prison (in some cases). I remember giving Dietrich Bonhoeffer's *Letters and Papers from Prison* to one such inmate. Newspaper headlines said that we were committing an offence against the *Crimes Act* because of our encouragement of opposition to conscription. I received dozens of telegrams from trade union leaders around Australia supporting our activities. I felt very secure. But more important was what was happening to those students involved in the Committee on Conscience. One of them said to me: 'This has been a cathartic experience.' Involved together with staff they, for the first time, shared experiences that could be life-shattering. In many ways it was the most memorable encounter I had ever had with students. I recall it vividly to this day.

Perhaps equal to this experience was another relating to refugee students after World War II. An organisation called World Student Relief (WSR) had been created in Europe to help university students who had become refugees. Many of them were bound for Australia. I first met some of them in Grindelwald in Switzerland in 1947.

Here some were gathered by WSR as a sort of rehabilitation in this beautiful alpine setting. I shared a room with a German student who had been captured by Australian troops in North Africa and sent to Canada as a prisoner of war. So at an earlier time in his life I would have been his enemy! That realisation left an indelible mark on my mind. When I returned to Australia WSR sent to me the names of students on each refugee boat arriving in Australia. Each one of them had a free passage, but was committed to work for the government for three years on assigned projects such as in a cement factory or similar manual work. Life was tough for them. A member of the staff of the Student Christian Movement, the saintly Rosalie McCutcheon, and I would meet these boats and make contact with the refugees and introduce them to fellow students in Australia as their first Australian contacts. They were helped eventually to continue university studies. Some did brilliantly. For others life problems were overwhelming and some committed suicide or ended up in mental hospitals. I have many stories. Here is just one. My secretary told me that a young man had turned up in a Cadillac and asked to see me. He said that many years before as a refugee student he had sought my advice. How could he become a student right away? My advice had been to learn English and earn some money first. He took my advice. He was now very wealthy, having spent these years, night and day, as the first manufacturer of nylon thread in Australia from its basic ingredients. He was now on his way to Pakistan to set up a plant there. He then told me he wanted to help a needy student whom I might know, in a sense pass on the favour. So I gave him a list!

Another outcome of my time at the University of California at Berkeley was one student who became interested in the philosophy of biology and bioethics. I discussed these issues in my course on evolution. Most were not interested but Charles Taylor was. He even came to Sydney for several months to learn more about Whitehead. His interest led him to become a leading researcher in artificial intelligence and artificial life at the University of California (Los Angeles) where he is a professor deeply concerned with the ethical issues these subjects raise. In the meantime he was a PhD student of Dobzhansky who also confronted him with questions in the philosophy of biology. We remain friends in contact to this day, though our emphases are different.

Going back to Berkeley, I had long discussions with Michael Lerner about ethical issues raised by modern genetics. He was convinced that these were critical issues of immediate concern. It was partly his concern that led me to meet Carl von Weizsäcker in Hamburg for advice, since Weizsäcker had been involved in the ethical issues raised by atomic energy. Under the auspices of the World Council of Churches we had a consultation in Zurich that included Michael Lerner and resulted in the book *Genetics and the Quality of Life* by Charles Birch and Paul Abrecht.

JBS Haldane

(Bassano and Vandyk Studios)

It is well to remember that in the 1920s biologists were divided into two camps. There were Darwinians and there were Mendelians. And they were at loggerheads. It took the work of three brilliant biologists, JBS Haldane and RA Fisher in the UK and Sewall Wright in the US, independently to show that a proper theory of evolution did not have to choose between Charles Darwin and Gregor Mendel, but could combine the two in a genetic theory of natural selection. Genetics provided both the maintenance of variability and the source of variability on which natural selection acted. It was one of the great discoveries of the century which led to the elaboration of the modern theory of evolution. All three discoverers provided convincing evidence by means of theoretical models. I discuss Sewall Wright later in this book. I only knew Fisher as the provider of statistical methods that ecologists and evolutionists find essential in their work. Sir Peter Medawar described Haldane as the cleverest man he ever knew. And Richard Lewontin said he had the most incisive and wide-ranging intellect he had ever known. I had a couple of interesting encounters with Haldane. The first time I visited him at University College in London in 1947 where he was professor of genetics. I was interested in the work he was doing on the fruit fly *Drosophila*. But I also wanted to tell him that his book *Possible Worlds* was very largely influential in my becoming a biologist. I had read it as a schoolboy and was intrigued by Haldane's ability to write so clearly and interestingly on so many areas in biology. Typical of these essays is one entitled 'Darwinism today' which begins with the quotation from Hilaire Belloc 'Darwinism is dead' only to show that Darwinism is very much alive. I had an hour or so with Haldane who then took me to a lower floor to meet his second wife Helen Spurway, a biologist in her own right. My second connection with Haldane was when he had moved to a statistical institute in India. I sought his advice on how to measure degrees of significance in a particular demographic index. His reply was helpful and his letter ended by suggesting to me that I would be better off in India because my Whiteheadian views were, he thought, akin to those of Hinduism. He himself then wore Indian dress and had ceased to eat meat. He called himself a Hindu atheist. Yet he was not a thorough going materialist whilst most of his biological colleagues were materialists. He said on one occasion that although we do not find obvious evidence of life or mind in so-called inert matter we can study them most easily when they are most completely manifested in human beings. We shall ultimately find them, he believed, at least in rudimentary form, all through the universe (see Waddington 1963 p 118). This is a Whiteheadian or pansubjective position rather rare amongst biologists. However, this was also true of evolutionary biologist CH Waddington (see pp. 32–33).

There are countless stories about Haldane many of which I have heard from two of his former students who worked in Australia; Jim Rendel one-time chief of the CSIRO Division of Animal Genetics and Michael White one-time professor of zoology in the University of Melbourne. Rendel I knew well as we were located in the same building in the University of Sydney for several years. I was delighted to discover that he was convinced of pansubjectivism. He owed his insight to no one but himself, at least so he said. Michael White was a strict mechanist so far as I could judge. Haldane was a friend of Aldous Huxley and is the biologist Shearwater in Huxley's novel *Antic Hay*. When asked 'Would you lay down you life to save your brother?' Haldane replied 'No. But I would to save two brothers or eight cousins.' The point being that you share 50 per cent of your genes with a brother and 12.5 per cent with a cousin.

Haldane wrote and recorded his own TV obituary, part of which was broadcast by the BBC. He died of cancer and wrote a poem soon after he was diagnosed. It was called 'Cancer is a funny thing.' In his self-obituary he concluded that what matters is not what people will think of him but what he's done, good or evil. He did much good. One common theme of this group of biologists was their interest in the philosophy of biology and particularly in the question: 'What is the origin and evolution of mentality?' And there are others who contribute to this question. So to it we shall return.

Conrad H Waddington

I had many discussions with Waddington (known to his colleagues as Wad) when he was director of the Institute of Genetics in the University of Edinburgh and we were both members of the executive committee of the International Institute of Biological Sciences. Waddington was its very energetic chairman. While together in a bookshop in Rome, when he was looking for a book on how to prune olive trees on his property on the Adriatic coast, he told me that as an undergraduate in Cambridge he had read all of Whitehead's works which are, for the most part, difficult to read. He pursued the same question as Haldane that if mind exists in the higher animals at what point in evolution did it originate? His conclusion was that it is inconceivable that it did not originate from anything that did not share something in common with it, but possessed only those qualities which can be objectively observed from outside. So we are forced to conclude, he says, that even in the simplest inanimate entities (eg, atoms) there is something akin to mentality. No system of electric currents, however complex, running through a complicated group of cells such as the brain can produce consciousness unless we allow that it is present at least as a potentiality in the elementary units of which the system is made (such as atoms and their components). Waddington did not get this insight from Haldane but from Whitehead. Waddington tells us that his philosophical views greatly influenced his research especially the subjects he chose to work on. When I discovered these were his views I was delighted to add him to my short list of biologists who had themselves found Whitehead's philosophy so illuminating.

While Waddington was an elder statesman of biology he was a great exponent of the new biology. In the 1960s we realised that zoology, botany, entomology and other disciplines centred on such groups of organisms that no longer reflected the reality of modern biology. Biology was now being sliced crosswise according to levels of biological organisation oriented to the molecule, cell, whole organism and the population. So appropriate subdivisions of biology would be cellular (including molecular) biology, organismic biology and population biology. When I came to press the case with the vice chancellor for a reorganisation of biology in the University of Sydney as a school of biological sciences I needed all the support I could muster. Waddington could help from a distance, but on the spot at the time was visiting professor Richard Lewontin, an ardent supporter of the project, so I was fortunate in being able to have him accompany me to the vice chancellor. He greatly helped in making a persuasive case for this reorganisation. I recall the somewhat reluctant vice chancellor pleading that he wanted to know who his professor of botany was when some embassy official confronted him with a weed from the embassy's garden for identification! Yet he agreed to the proposition of a school of biological science made from existing departments.

Sewall Wright

Sewall Wright was one of the founders of the modern evolutionary synthesis also known as neo-Darwinism. His contribution was largely theoretical and mathematical in contrast to that of Dobzhansky who combined experimental work both in the laboratory and the field. In some studies he collaborated with Dobzhansky. They wrote five papers together. Wright's distinction as an evolutionary biologist is indicated by his being the only member of the zoology department in the University of Chicago with the title of Distinguished Service Professor. He published his first scientific paper at the age of 23 and his last when he was 99 in 1988, the year of his death. He also had the distinction of having published his first book *Evolution and the Genetics of Populations* at the age of nearly 80. It became a four-volume set within the decade 1968–78 and is now a classic. It was on one of his customary long walks that he slipped on the icy footpath and fractured his pelvis. He died a few days later from pulmonary embolism.

I came to know Sewall Wright when I spent a year in the

zoology department at the University of Chicago in 1946 and later at two symposia on science and philosophy in Bellagio, Italy. He was a quiet and unassuming scientist who had the reputation of being absent minded. He had the habit when lecturing (which I witnessed) of filling the blackboard with equations. As his right hand wrote the equations his left hand rubbed them out at the same rate. On one occasion it is said that he had in his pocket one of his experimental guinea pigs which he withdrew and absent-mindedly used as an eraser. He lectured from a pack of three-inch by five-inch cards which sometimes got muddled up. He was usually behind in his planned course of lectures. Near the end of the quarter, on his way to a class, he admitted that so far he had covered half the course and was giving the other half that day.

Of special interest to me was Sewall Wright's philosophy of biology. In contrast to Dobzhansky and pretty well most other biologists he supported the concept of panpsychism or pansubjectivism. Most biologists think that mind in evolution arose from no-mind. At some stage in evolution mind appeared when it did not exist before. Wright argued that to believe that mind rose from no-mind is to believe in miracles. The property of mind must exist all down the line to, and including, the fundamental physical particles, a view which he got from the 19th century English philosopher WK Clifford via the English statistician Karl Pearson's *The Grammar of Science* and later from Whitehead. Wright was saddened that his philosophical views received almost no attention from biologists. On the other hand it attracted some attention from philosophers and notably from a professor of philosophy in the University of Chicago, namely Charles Hartshorne. They became life-long friends. Hartshorne had a graduate student, who was working on pansubjectivism, with whom I had some discussions which resulted in my being invited to see 'Mr and Mrs Hartshorne at home June 5th 1946 from four to six 124 East 57th Street.' So for me also began a life-long friendship with Charles and Dorothy Hartshorne.

Wright and Hartshorne recognised an outer and inner aspect of things. It is obvious that in addition to what others recognise in us as our outer aspects, such as the colour of our eyes, we are aware of an inner aspect (which represents our feelings or consciousness). This is the first-person view of ourselves. The third-person view of ourselves is what others observe about us. Pansubjectivism attributes an inner aspect not just to animals, but to the sequence of entities from fundamental particles to molecules to cells and so on to humans. Wright argued that whereas a previous generation saw an unbridgeable gap between supposedly non-living molecules and living cells this gap is being bridged by such entities as the gene. Wright then gives his arguments in which he regards the gene as like a living organism rather than an inanimate machine.

This turns on its head the traditional view that all the entities from quarks to humans are machines that have no inner or subjective aspect. In modern times René Descartes gave us this 'Cartesian' view of things. All these entities are machines. It is one thing to say that they are all like machines. It is quite another to say they are machines. The great advances of science have been made by supposing that the entities scientists study are like machines, for science studies the outer aspect of things. The heart in its aspect which the physiologist studies is like a pump. The brain and its mind is like a clock. Updating the metaphor from clocks to computers still utilises the machine analogy. In carrying out this program the scientist should not deceive himself or others into thinking that he is giving an account of all reality. The inner aspect of everything escapes him. Wright and Hartshorne were concerned with how to include this inner aspect in a vision of reality. The classical physicist, for example, can only tell us that electrons repel one another according to a certain law. He says nothing about their real being and knows that he cannot. The discoverer of the electron JJ Thomson said that to know an electron you would have to be one. That expresses a view of the inner aspect of things which the modern quantum physicist is coming to recognise as, for example, in the work of David Bohm. Bohm argues that quantum theory undermines the assumption of mechanism. He distinguishes the outer aspects of nature, which classical physics studies as the explicate order, and the inner aspect of things as the implicate order. There is no thing in the universe. All is process. He anticipated that the first-person felt experience and the third-person description will both become part of an extended form of scientific method. While physics is moving away from mechanism, biology and psychology are moving closer to it. Such a position cannot last.

Bohm had a remarkable personality. I met him at two conferences on the philosophy of biology at the beautiful Villa Serbelloni at Bellagio on Lake Como under the auspices of the Rockefeller Foundation. The villa is more like a palace and a wonderful place to meet. Bohm was charismatic and self-giving with a wonderfully persuasive way of speaking. I have the most vivid memories of his community presence. His charm and originality eventually led to his becoming a guru, which was, in a way, inevitable.

There is a second reason why the picture the scientist draws of reality is partial. We are in a sense imprisoned in a way precisely expressed by physicist Werner Heisenberg's famous remark that we do not see nature as it is, but only as a consequence of the questions we put to it.

Wright began his scientific career as a strict mechanist. This position was shaken when he read Henri Bergson's *Creative Evolution*. Then came a famous dispute in Chicago between Jacques Loeb and HS Jennings on the interpretation of animal behaviour. Loeb was the arch mechanist who invented a mechanical insect that followed him with his torch around the lab. Loeb is portrayed as the mechanistic scientist Max Gottlieb in Sinclair Lewis's novel *Arrowsmith*. Jennings suggested that if an Amoeba were the size of a dog we would attribute to it the sorts of feelings we attribute to a dog. Wright found himself somewhat in sympathy with Jennings' position. However it was in AN Whitehead's *Science and the Modern World* that Wright found the most complete philosophical development of the organic view of nature; Whitehead called it organic mechanism. I also became convinced of the organic view of nature through reading the same book.

So here we have in Sewall Wright and Dobzhansky two famous evolutionists with contrasting views on the nature of nature they investigated. One sees nature primarily in terms of mechanism with the non-mechanistic feature of mind emerging from no mentality somewhere in the evolution of the vertebrates. The other sees mentality as a central feature of all entities from humans down to quarks. One sees the world primarily as made of machines. The other sees the world primarily in terms of mental events. One is dualistic or materialistic. The other is monistic and non-materialistic. We shall try to give some reasons later on as to why most biologists (perhaps most people who think about it) are materialistic and believe that mind evolved from no mind. Cogent and detailed arguments in support of the view that mind cannot evolve from no mind are given by David Griffin (1998 p 64). More about this and its importance is discussed in Chapters 5 and 6. It is quite evident from the above that I learned a lot from Sewall

Wright about the concept of mentality as existing in some form all the way down to quarks. Why this is so important I pursue in Chapters 5 and 6.

Wilfred E Agar

(Optical Munitions with WE Agar, Registration No 123, The Physics Museum, University of Melbourne)

Bvo!! Epigenetics Rat Tails woops!

Wilfred E Agar was the professor of zoology at the University of Melbourne from 1920 to 1948. He was a distinguished cell biologist, but is probably best known for his experiment with rats demonstrating that acquired characters are not inherited. As a first year student in 1936 I well recall his lectures on animal behaviour, a subject only then coming into prominence. As was the case with all professors in Australian universities at that time he hailed from England. Each department had just one professor who was known as *the professor*. Agar came from King's College, Cambridge, and was a fellow of the Royal Society. I didn't appreciate that he was deeply interested in the philosophy of biology until 1949 when he gave an address to science students on 'Some philosophical problems in biology'. I had at that stage read Whitehead's *Science and the Modern World* so I was delighted to find in his address his Whiteheadian view of nature. He said that philosophical problems arise when refusing to regard oneself merely as an external spectator (the third-person point of view) of nature, one takes seriously the fact that each of us has a first-person view of nature through our feelings. One then asks: 'How far from humans down the line is there subjectivity?' In Agar's view the universe is psycho-physical throughout.

Agar's lecture was given at the University of Melbourne. So I wrote to him on behalf of the student Science Association in the University of Adelaide where I then was. We invited him to address students in Adelaide. I received from him a hand written letter dated 25 July 1949 which I have kept. He was unable to accept our invitation because of ill health. He said in part:

> I was quite overwhelmed by your invitation ... will you please convey my grateful thanks to the other signatories of the letter of invitation which I shall preserve among my most treasured possessions as the most cordial expression of good will I have ever received from my fellow biologists.

His letter made me realise for the first time that even the famous like to be appreciated. Even the great Darwin wrote in his autobiography that he wanted a 'fair place among scientific men'.

I had been in touch with Agar earlier to ask him whom I should read on the philosophy of biology. He suggested Charles Hartshorne's *The Philosophy and Psychology of Sensation* which began my renewed interest in Hartshorne. Much later Hartshorne wrote in *The Philosophy of Charles Hartshorne* vol XX 'The Library of Living Philosophers':

Although my book *The Philosophy and Psychology of Sensation* scored no great success in this country or in England: it achieved one success in Australia that was fortunate for me. It appealed to the professor of zoology at the University of Melbourne, WE Agar who convinced his student Charles Birch, that my book, as an application of Whitehead's philosophy, was significant for biological theory.

Agar had also recommended to me his own forthcoming book modestly titled *A Contribution to the Theory of the Living Organism* (1943). Its first sentence reads 'The main thesis of this book is that all living organisms are subjects.' The characteristic of a subject is that it is a feeling or experiencing being. This is, to say the least, an unusual way of commencing a study of living organisms. Having established that all living organisms are like humans in this respect he then interpolates this view all the way down to atoms. In the process Agar deals with three big issues in biology: animal behaviour, development (embryology) and evolution. He seeks to show how Whitehead's philosophy of organism and the notion of purpose is relevant to a proper understanding of these disciplines. A rather unkind review in the *Journal of Philosophy* by Ernest Nagel dampened somewhat interest in its reception. As with Agar's exposition of his philosophy Hartshorne's was also ignored by biologists except for his work on bird-song. It seems that adventurist philosophical physicists get a better reception from their colleagues than do adventurist biologists from theirs. One reason is that biology is still living in the age of mechanism as *de rigueur* whereas physics has been jolted out of simple mechanism by quantum physics.

In recent years molecular biologists have turned their attention to investigating consciousness or mind. The techniques for doing this were unavailable in Agar's day. Would he have been happy with their approach? So far as it goes perhaps, but it does not go far enough. It is fascinating to know in what regions of the brain we experience the colour red and what electrical impulses in the nerves are characteristic of this experience. They are what is called biological correlates of the experience. They are objective aspects of consciousness. The subjective aspects of experience still elude the investigator. How to overcome this problem is discussed later in this book. Agar established a strong case for trying to overcome this omission well ahead of his time. But it has yet to be taken up seriously by biologists. Agar's thought greatly influenced my own and reinforced the conviction I was developing of the importance of the process thought of AN Whitehead for biology.

2 ANIMAL ECOLOGISTS

The word *oecologie* was coined by the German biologist Ernst Haeckel in 1870. Its root is the Greek word *oikos* meaning home. *Oecologie* or the English *ecology* is about the life of living organisms in their homes. What we recognise as ecological studies go back earlier such as, for example, Charles Darwin's studies on what he called the struggle for existence. Some claim that Theophrastos was an ecologist, he succeeded Aristotle as leader of the Lyceum in Athens. He associated particular plants with particular habitats such as marshes, shallow water or deep water.

Since ecology has to do with the relationship of organisms to their environment one might have thought that ecologists would be interested in a philosophy of relationships such as process thought, but this is not the case. They have (for the most part) followed Darwin in mechanistic thinking. This is more often implied rather than explicit and is characteristic of ecologists that are discussed in this section.

Historically the ecology of animals has proceeded somewhat independently of the study of the ecology of plants. Charles Elton was the founder of the modern science of animal ecology in the UK. Arthur Tansley was the founder of plant ecology in the UK. He coined the word 'ecosystem' in 1935 for the study of all the organisms and their environments in specified habitats, such as lakes. The ecosystem included plants, animals, micro-organisms and any other living organisms, the water and its sediments and the relation between them all. However, this concept is problematic, as the ecosystem has no clear boundaries. Many of the inhabitants of a lake, for example, such as some insects live part of their lives as larvae in the water and as adults a long way beyond its shores. The word 'ecosystem' has been bandied about by environmentalists to label anything they want to preserve, such as a coral reef; when the simple word 'habitat' might be more appropriate. A central idea of plant ecology is plant succession. Many times I have visited the Indiana sand dunes at the southern end of Lake Michigan with students from the University of Chicago. A classic example of plant succession from the lake-shore to the maple-beech climax forest further inland was initially studied by FE Clements. The animal ecologists came in after to find that the different sequences in the plant succession were occupied by different animals. Fortunately, for me, Charles Hartshorne had a small cottage in the maple-beech woods, where he studied the birds and particularly their song. I visited him there on occasions and learned a lot about aesthetics of bird-song as well as ecology. I was always amazed that such lovely woods existed so close to the huge city of Chicago to the north and the huge Indiana steel mills visible to the south. We can thank conservationists for its preservation. My own studies have been primarily on the population ecology of animals, especially insects and to some extent on human ecology (see Andrewartha and Birch 1954 and 1984).

Charles Elton

(Courtesy of Charles Birch)

Charles Elton was the founder of the modern science of animal ecology. When I first knew Elton he was director and founder (in 1932) of an ecological centre in Oxford University with the curious name Bureau of Animal Population. He wanted it to be a centre of ecological information as well as research. The place was full of filing cabinets chock-a-block with reprints of ecological studies. It was a centre where ecologists came to exchange ideas, write books or stayed for longer periods to do research. I fell into the latter category, arriving in 1947 after my year at the University of Chicago. Elton we called Charles, though he tended to call us by un-prefixed surnames. First names only started to be used in Oxford in the 1940s. Post-war rationing of food and clothing still existed. Some items were in short supply. Knowing this I packed a food parcel in Chicago of such items as coffee and butter which I gave to Elton on my arrival. He looked embarrassed and simply said with a stiff upper lip: 'We can manage alright.' Modest, unassuming, courageous with ideas, and basically friendly, but in ways so different from the Chicagoans I had got used to. He introduced me to PH Leslie his statistician, who had read a recent paper of mine. Leslie thoughtfully suggested that my analysis could be improved by using concepts from demography, which had been developed further. Much of the year I spent with him in discussion and revising my paper. He was very generous with his time. This was true of others at the bureau including graduate students. I became aware of a huge difference of the approach to time in England and the US. Take one example: graduate students. In the US, graduate students keep their lights burning well into the night. The day was well spent if it was never ending. Their mistake was to confuse hard work with hard thinking. There was the ever-present coffee pot to keep one awake and regular visits to the psychiatrist. Rarely was communal morning or afternoon coffee celebrated with others. In Oxford, by comparison, graduate students rarely arrived before 10 in the morning and soon after that had morning tea with others. This was an opportunity to discuss work including new discoveries from journals. Lunch would usually be a long drawn out affair. And soon after would come high tea with cream buns. The atmosphere was relaxed. I got the impression that the English graduate student achieved in one hour what took three or four hours in the US. If anyone had a shrink no one knew about it. The culture of the famous Cavendish laboratory in Cambridge in Ernest Rutherford's time had similar elements. Rutherford put strict limits on the hours his students kept. Every evening at six o'clock the laboratory was closed and all work had to stop. Four times every year the laboratory was closed for two weeks of vacation. Rutherford believed that scientists would be more creative if they spent the evenings relaxing with their families and enjoying frequent holidays. It seemed to pay off. An extraordinary high proportion of his students eventually won Nobel Prizes. They were of course a pretty bright bunch of 20th century students. They stood in contrast to the famous 19th century British scientists who were cultured gentlemen with adequate private means such as, for example, Charles Darwin and Joseph Banks.

One day Elton came into my laboratory beaming; he had just made a remarkable discovery. He found three scientists in Oxford each working on vitamin B but none of them knew that each other existed. And said Elton: 'Isn't that wonderful!' I am not sure what the moral of that story is other than that remarkable things happen at Oxford.

In the 1940s animal ecology was only just being recognised as a valid science. The central study of zoology since Darwin's time was comparative anatomy, which was supposed to pile up evidence for evolution; making it the way to understand anatomical differences and similarities in animals. Oxford zoology felt it was stretching the limit when it agreed to have a course on animal ecology. Years later in 1960 Elton wrote to me 'It is interesting to see how ecology is gradually holding people's interest though biochemistry and physiology, with their nice neat experiments are still so popular. Yet you hardly ever see an ecological paper in the Royal Society Proceedings.' This seemed to be a British phenomenon. Ecology was then well established in university courses in the US. When I joined the staff of the zoology department at the University of Sydney in 1948 the professor, WJ Dakin, was an Englishman and marine biologist. He asked me to teach a course on comparative physiology. I turned it into a course on ecological physiology which was acceptable to the professor. When I suggested that I go the whole hog and have a course in animal ecology he told me to go easy on that. Although Eric Ashby (later Lord Ashby) had been teaching plant ecology in the botany department, the idea of animal ecology had not caught on as an academic subject. It seemed a messy sort of area. Someone, I recall at the time, even called it a manure heap.

Elton wrote the first major text on animal ecology called *Animal Ecology* when he was 27 in the year 1927. It established principles of the subject including the concepts of food chain, pyramid of numbers, ecological niche, the ecological community and animal numbers. It was clear and precise and became a classic, which it remains to this day. When Andrewartha and I wrote our text on animal ecology *The Distribution and Abundance of Animals* in 1954 our title came from Elton's book in which he called animal ecology 'the distribution and numbers of animals in nature'.

Elton was first and foremost a naturalist. He wanted to know about animals in nature. His first lecture to Oxford students on animal ecology began with a slide on the screen showing a young ecologist with a knapsack on his back and a net in his hand. Most days Elton rode his bicycle to Wytham Woods near Oxford. He was getting ideas for his next book on animal communities. I asked him if I could accompany him one day to find out what he was doing in the field. He said no as he was not sure what he was doing! I never did go with him. But one day he showed me a reed he had brought back. An insect had been feeding on the reed. It did not chew the stem in half but made regular bites along the length of the stem without cutting the veins so that in no place was the stem completely chewed through. So the stem still survived the insect's ravages. 'What do you make of that?' he asked. On another occasion he walked into the lab after a morning at Wytham Woods and asked me: 'What examples do you know of animals influencing the succession of plants?' He had got some ideas from what he had seen that morning.

I did visit another wood near Oxford with ornithologist David Lack and his students. They were counting the number of a certain owl in the woods. This was done by stationing the students and myself equally spaced in the wood each with a notebook to record the time of each owl hoot. Putting the records together it was possible to estimate the number of owls. However, my records had to be discounted because I had recorded too many hoots which evidently included train hoots from Oxford railway station. On the next visit I paid for my misdemeanours. I was persuaded to climb a tree to count the number of baby storks in the nest on top. Just within reach they all put their necks over for me to count and promptly vomited in my face, to the great mirth of the students at the bottom of the tree.

Elton was instrumental in bringing to conservation a scientific understanding that took into account human needs and the wellbeing of nature. It meant looking for some wise principle of co-existence between humanity and nature, even if it had to be a modified kind of humanity and a modified kind of nature. This was my introduction to conservation, which had become an important subject by the time I returned to Australia in 1948. Australia had the distinction of having one of the highest rates of extinction of animals in the world and its agriculture was already becoming unsustainable as it spread further and further into the dry inland. The fate of plants and animals was to become an important focus in my worldview.

Herbert George Andrewartha

HG Andrewartha (known as Andy) was on the staff of the Waite Agricultural Research Institute in Adelaide when I became his first research student. Indeed I was only the second research student at the Waite Institute. This I learned from the director the day I began. He added that the first one was a failure! The Waite Institute was modelled on the famous Rothamsted Agricultural Research Institute in England. The Waite Institute had become a mecca for the science of agriculture in Australia.

Andrewartha was a great admirer of Charles Elton, particularly for his workman-like approach to ecology. Further Elton had a straightforward way of writing which greatly appealed to Andrewartha who insisted that his own research students learn to write with clarity. He achieved this with suggestions for reading and in particular he advocated Somerset Maugham's book *The Summing Up*, which in its early pages argued that one must aim at lucidity, simplicity and euphony in that order of importance. He pointed out that there are two sorts of obscurity, one is due to negligence and the other to wilfulness. In the first case people never take the trouble to learn to write clearly. In the second case some writers just can't think clearly and are inclined to suppose that their thoughts have a significance greater than appears at first sight. It is flattering to believe that they are too profound to be expressed so clearly that all who run may read. It is a dire sin for academics to suggest to their students, as some do today, that obscurity and complexity are acceptable, even desirable. We need clarity and simplicity. Ecological writings are often verbose and abstract. Yet science as a whole has fostered simplicity and clarity in writing. Way back the Royal Society had put the poet John Dryden on its committee to teach scientists a simple and direct style for writing English.

Like Elton, Andrewartha was first and foremost a naturalist. His own large garden and the surrounding bush were constant sources of delight for the mind of the naturalist. So it was inevitable that he spent a lot of his time in the field. This brought him, for example, into the semi-desert outback of South Australia to study the plague grasshopper. On one occasion, Andrewartha and his wife Vevers did not arrive back in Adelaide as expected. The head of the department, Professor James Davidson, asked the Australian Broadcasting Commission to send out a request for information about their whereabouts, which they did during a radio broadcast of a Test Cricket Match: Australia versus England. The broadcast said that Andrewartha and his wife were last seen at Mount Hopeless!

Andrewartha was a personality of strong convictions. He appreciated being in the entomology department headed by Professor James Davidson. Davidson was one of two foundation professors of the Waite Institute from Rothamsted who laid the foundations of much population ecology of insects in Australia. Andrewartha believed in the supremacy of science as a way of thinking. This was new for me. I had not really discovered what science was while an undergraduate and moreover I had strong religious convictions. Andrewartha was the first person to challenge my ideas. I came to think that my foundations were of sand. In my search for answers I found resolution in AN Whitehead's thoughts in *Science and the Modern World* which introduced me to a liberal view of Christianity that I had not known existed. Andrewartha was not too impressed with my discovery. Although Whitehead was a scientist of great distinction, he was a philosopher whose philosophy was metaphysical. I remember Andrewartha saying to me that perhaps there was room for one Whitehead in the world, but certainly not more. However, he was happy to join in a regular discussion group on social and political issues of the Student Christian Movement (SCM) that I introduced him to. He did comment on discussion being concluded by what the SCM called a devotional. He said we seemed to have two bowsers: one that was rational and the second which was irrational, invoking some outside source.

I am deeply indebted to Andrewartha for teaching me how to think, something I never learned as an undergraduate. Secondly, he led me to discovering the social responsibility of the scientist. In view of the enormous transformation of the modern world as a result of science and technology the scientist is responsible for much that has happened both good and bad. This understanding is based on the premise that science is not value free. The assessment of evidence is not value free. The goals of science are not value free. Half of the scientists and engineers in the industrial nations are employed in the development of weapons. The threat of a nuclear holocaust carries with it responsibility on those whose science contributed to nuclear weapons. A similar responsibility lies with those whose science contributes to global warming. It is antediluvian to suppose that scientists produce value-free data that is handed over to politicians to value and use.

Andrewartha and I together wrote two large books on animal ecology. They both challenged the dominant views of the time. Both were published by the University of Chicago Press. I recall vividly when I presented the manuscript of *The Distribution and Abundance of Animals* (1954) to Professor Thomas Park, who was on the board of the press, he commented: 'I hope the press does not lose its shirt over this one.' Well they didn't and must have made quite a handsome profit over many years of reprinting including paperback editions. Our second ecological text was *The Ecological Web* (1984) with the subtitle *More on the Distribution and Abundance of Animals*.

Looking back I can recall just two times when I had a sense of insecurity in my work. The first was when Andrewartha was my supervisor in research. I had very good project on the influence of temperature and moisture on the development of the eggs of a plague grasshopper. My first project. But was I capable of doing it or would Andrewartha think I was an incompetent idiot? Well he didn't seem to think so. The second time was when I began work with Dobzhansky at Columbia University. Would he like me or regard me as second rate? So I asked the chairman of the department, John Moore, for advice. He replied 'once Dobzhansky decides he likes you he will continue to like and support you. In fact he likes you.' So that was encouraging. St Francis of Assisi learned that a young friar was suffering from the fear that Francis his hero really despised him. Francis walked up to the young man who was silent and grave and said:

Be not troubled in your thoughts for you are dear to me, and even among the number of those who are most dear. You know that you are worthy of my friendship and society; therefore come to me, in confidence whensoever you will, and from friendship learn faith [Chesterton 1934 p 121].

Although Andrewartha had a great admiration for Elton and both had quite strong views in their interpretation of ecology there were some major differences. Andrewartha gathered around him graduate students and post-doctorals who tended to agree with everything Andrewartha said. You always knew where they stood. By contrast Elton's group was diverse. And in his lectures he would present all sides and leave it to the listener's own judgment on the relative merits of each case. I think I stood somewhere in between. I never had the unswerving admiration from my students such as Andy's students had for his views and which they tended to promote in their later life-work. I admired Andrewartha for this and did not quite know why I was different.

The two books we wrote together were a consensus of our views. By contrast, in *Principles of Animal Ecology* by WC Allee, Alfred Emerson, Orlando Park, Thomas Park and Karl Schmidt (1949), each chapter represented the views of the author who wrote it. While they were writing they met each Sunday morning to discuss each author's efforts for the week. I saw them doing this but had no inkling of what was going on.

Elton recognised a difference between his attitude and that of his long-time colleague Dennis Chitty, who did much work on cycles of numbers in mammals such as voles. In a letter Elton wrote to Chitty, which Chitty published, Elton predicted that Chitty would more and more live in a team-world of his own with people around him who agreed with every word he said. It was pretty strong medicine given from the boss to a member of his staff.

Thomas Park

(Courtesy of Charles Birch)

There was a second difference from Elton which Andrewartha and I shared. Elton had much admiration for experimental models of ecology typically represented by the 'Tribolium model' of Thomas Park of Chicago. *Tribolium* is a flour beetle. His studies on 'competition' between different species are typical examples of this model. I gave a seminar in Elton's bureau on experimental studies I had done with two grain weevils. It was all fairly simple stuff yet Elton speaking to me afterwards expressed great admiration that such experiments could be done, perhaps because he had never done any. This is further indicated by Elton's dedication of his book *The Pattern of Animal Communities* (1966) to Thomas Park. Andrewartha and I questioned what relevance the *Tribolium* model might have for natural populations. If you were to ask why I did such experiments I would reply that they pointed to some of the interactions between species at high densities and probably told more about evolution than ecology. Andrewartha and my models of natural populations were much more complex than simple experimental ones in the laboratory. The attraction of some ecologists to the simple models is that they may serve to demonstrate with real animals what mathematical models predict. And there are plenty of ecologists who believe that nature is like the simple models. This is an ongoing dispute amongst ecologists. Professor Bob May (now Lord May of Oxford), a leading theoretical modeller said to me that if the simple mathematical models turn out to be correct models of nature then that is a big win worth aiming at. I thought the chances of winning that game were pretty low.

Thomas Park of the University of Chicago was one of the authors of *Principles of Animal Ecology*. I worked in his lab for a year as Chicago was then a world centre in animal ecology. Besides Park there was WC Allee (animal aggregations), Alfred Emerson (termites) and Sewall Wright (genetics). Park used the term 'population ecology' to define the studies he was making and of others that concentrated on numbers of animals. Park made the flour beetle *Tribolium* an ecological model much as research on the fruit fly *Drosophila* was a model for genetics. I doubt that he was original in his ideas, but he did have an uncanny ability to bring concepts together that gave the impression that population ecology was emerging as a science with its own principles. This made him an exceptionally good lecturer. He would fill the blackboard in advance with a list of headings of subjects he would be dealing with. These days the students would demand that all this be put on PowerPoints and relayed to their own computers.

Paul and Anne Ehrlich

(Courtesy of Paul and Anne Ehrlich)

Elton proposed that in order to conserve life we had to discover some new principle of coexistence between humanity and nature, even if it had to be a modified kind of humanity and nature. Paul and Anne Ehrlich (who are as active today as they ever have been), have discovered such a principle and helped to put it into practice. They have been a continuing influence on me since we first met at the International Congress of Zoology in Washington DC in 1963. This was to be the last meeting of the International Congress of Zoology which recognised that there was less credence in the modern world for a science of animals (zoology) and another of plants (botany) and another of microbes (microbiology). These categories were to be subsumed in a biology of three different levels: cells, organisms and populations. Ever since that meeting the Ehrlichs have visited Australia almost every year. They have had ecological projects in Australia, two of their former students occupying professorial chairs in Australian universities and we have always had ecological issues to discuss.

I never had an overall way of picturing the environmental impact of humanity until they developed with John Holdren the quantitative formula for environmental impact:

- Environmental Impact = Population x Affluence x Technology or
- I = PAT where A and T = per person.

Each of these components can in principle be measured. Affluence, for example, can be measured as units of energy per person. T might be measured in terms of grams of sulphur per kilowatt hour of energy per person. The effect of environmental impact is threefold. It threatens the life-support systems of the Earth. It is a cause of extinction of species and a corresponding reduction in biodiversity. It results in a reduction of the resources of the Earth that are needed by humans and other species. To achieve any reduction of environmental impact will involve a change in values that humans espouse, a transcending of individualism, anthropocentrism, mechanism, consumerism, nationalism and militarism.

There is perhaps no more striking quantitative estimate of environmental impact than the estimate made by the Ehrlich group that the human economy uses directly and indirectly 40 per cent of the terrestrial primary production of plant material produced every year. Primary terrestrial plant production is the total production of plants in forests, grasslands and crops. This view has not been challenged.

The Ehrlichs' diagnosis and cure for the Earth's ills has been widely recognised by virtue of their skills in communication. Paul was such a big hit on the late-night Johnny Carson show on television that his appearances were classified as entertainment and he was required to register in the Actors Guild. I recall what must have been one of his earliest talks to a business group in San Francisco. The talk was entitled 'Food from the Sea – a Red Herring'. It got headlines in the San Francisco papers. His speaking style is like Niagara Falls; impact after impact with no breath in between. With a couple of books published every year the Ehrlichs have made a tremendous impression on the whole subject of population biology. The above is merely an introduction to that impact.

Environmental ethicists

Environmental ethics needs to be informed by valid science. Ecologists are naturally concerned about having their science distorted by environmentalists when they make claims such as 'complexity enhances stability' that do not necessarily reflect a current disciplinary consensus.

What I have learned about environmental ethics has come primarily from John Cobb and David Griffin of the Center for Process Studies in Claremont, California. Two sorts of value are recognised in process thought: instrumental (or extrinsic value) and intrinsic value. The argument that is dominant in conservation circles for the preservation of nature is to look after nature because nature looks after us. This is a recognition of the instrumental value of nature. There are four sorts of instrumental value in nature:

- the preservation of species that are useful to us;
- the preservation of species for experimental purposes;
- the use of nature for leisure; and
- the 'cathedral argument' of preservation of nature for aesthetic purposes.

In all these values plants and animals are seen as ends for human purposes or for the wellbeing of other species.

Beside their instrumental value to us and other organisms, each individual animal has intrinsic value. It is the value something has in and for itself. What then gives this value to an individual? The answer first became clear to me in discussions with John Cobb and David Griffin. The only things that are anything for themselves are, of course, entities with experience. It is feelings that give intrinsic value. There might be widespread agreement that it is feelings in humans that makes us respect individual people. But there is widespread dispute as to how far down the scale – from humans to cats and dogs to snakes to single cells such as Amoeba to atoms and so on – we recognised entities with feelings. Some make the cut off with birds, others with crayfish. But pansubjectivism makes no dividing line at all: the subjective exists all down the line, in some form analogous to what we call feelings in ourselves but not necessarily conscious feelings. We cannot know the experience of another person. We do not have their experience, which is private and theirs alone. We can only infer by analogy.

From what has been said it follows that in nature there is a gradation of intrinsic value. Not all entities have the same intrinsic value. A human has more intrinsic value than a mosquito because it is reasonable to suppose that a human being has a greater richness of experience than a mosquito. This is because a human being has greater freedom, self-reflection, capacity to wonder, creativity and communication. Furthermore only humans have a moral responsibility to other organisms. The capacity for richness of experience in different animals is probably related to the development of the nervous system.

The ethical imperative that follows from the recognition of intrinsic value is that creatures besides ourselves make an ethical claim upon us. This is a biocentric as opposed to an anthropocentric ethic. We deal with living organisms appropriately when we rightly balance their intrinsic value with their instrumental value. One example will suffice. The European Union officially recognised in June 1997 that animals have feelings. Changes to the EU's basic treaty arrangements now require that EU rules on agriculture, trade, transport and scientific research pay full regard to the welfare of animals as sentient beings. We then restore a lost feeling for nature which William Wordsworth described in his familiar sonnet:

> The world is too much with us; late and soon,
> Getting and spending, we lay waste our powers;
> Little we see in Nature that is ours;
> We have given our hearts away, a sordid boon!
> The Sea that bares her bosom to the moon,
> The winds that will be howling at all hours,
> And are up-gather'd now like sleeping flowers;
> For this for everything, we are out of tune;
> It moves us not – Great God! I'd rather be
> A pagan suckled in a creed outworn;
> So might I, standing on this pleasant lea;
> Have glimpses that would make me less forlorn;
> Have sight of Proteus rising from the sea;
> Or hear old Triton blow his wreathed horn.

Proteus and Triton are examples of what we have lost, the capacity to see ourselves and our moods in nature, to relate to nature's intrinsic value as a dimension of our own experience.

The ethical conclusions of animal rightists and environmental ethicists do not always coincide. Animal rightists have opposed the elimination of feral goats that have ruined the habitats of islands over much of the Earth. The environmental ethicist in these situations calls for an assessment of the negative instrumental value of the feral animals against their intrinsic value, whereas the animal liberationist is primarily concerned with the intrinsic value of the animals concerned. The liberationist is anxious to avoid suffering or reduce it to a minimum. This environmental ethic becomes part of my understanding of meaning in life, which is developed in Chapters 5 and 6.

3 PHILOSOPHERS OF RELIGION

Being asked, 'Which are more important, facts or ideas?' AN Whitehead reflected a while, then said 'Ideas about facts' (Price 1954 p 337). Facts are the world's data. Theories are structures of ideas that explain and interpret facts. Evolution is a theory. It is also a fact. The important *facts* for Whitehead came from science and secondly from the experience of living. The important *ideas* for Whitehead came from his search for meaning to tie facts together. It is true that there are people who are casual about facts and who appear not to be concerned with a search for meaning. Indeed the Australian playwright David Williamson says of the citizens of my own city Sydney in his play *Emerald City*: 'No-one in Sydney ever wastes time debating the meaning of life – it's getting yourself a water frontage' says one of his characters. Some are mightily confused. Professor David Armstrong's lectures on René Descartes to students at the University of Sydney included this story: a philosophy lecturer noticed one of his students looking more and more worried as the course progressed. The student was absent for a while, then staggered in unkempt, dirty and tired. 'Professor, professor' he said. 'You've got to help me. *Do I really exist?*' The professor looked around and said 'Who wants to know?' (Franklin 2003 p 111).

While it may be true that well-to-do Sydneysiders are more interested in searching for a waterfront, there are intelligent people who, left to themselves, will philosophise sooner or later about the meaning of their lives. They need help. Philosopher David Stove puts it this way:

> Take Professor AB, our distinguished geneticist, member of such-and-such, winner of the so-and-so, what a clever man *he* must be! Well, so he is, in a way, but he is no glassy way essence of genetic knowledge; he is lots of other things as well, and one of them is that he happens to be a Methodist half-wit. Or take CD, a top physicist; but he also happens to take Uri Geller seriously, or believes that the latest physics vindicates Berkeley's spiritual philosophy. Professor EF of pure mathematics, approaching retirement, begins to drive his busy colleagues wild by asking questions like 'what the hell are numbers, anyway?' [Franklin 2003 p 432]

And so one could go on. It so happens Stove's examples are professors, but they could be any of us. We need help to fit the various elements of our lives into a consistent meaning. Science and religion are two critical elements.

Whitehead's ideas on the meaning of life challenge much contemporary thought that is materialistic; much of it derived from an interpretation of science that excludes knowledge not based on scientific fact. Karl Popper drew what he considered to be the boundaries of science. Anything outside that boundary was interpreted by some as not being knowledge. I asked Popper if he thought that science was the only avenue to truth. He answered with an emphatic 'no'. The famous fifth chapter in Whitehead's *Science and the Modern World* entitled 'The Romantic Reaction' is about the reaction of the poets to exclusive materialism as the central idea about the universe. Whitehead went on to say that the only way of mitigating materialism is by the discovery that it is not materialism. William Wordsworth's characteristic thought was summed up in the phrase 'We murder to dissect.' And Alfred Tennyson wrote:

> Flower in the crannied wall,
> I pluck you out of the crannies –
> Hold you here, root and all, in my hand.
> Little flower – but if I could understand
> What you are, root and all, and all in all,
> I should know what God and man is.

The poet contrasts this with the scientist who 'botanises on his mother's grave'. What moved the poets was that they felt something had been left out of a mechanistic universe, and what had been left out comprised everything that was most important. What was denied were values, change, organism, in a word 'feelings'. I recall walking with theologian Reinhold Niebuhr in New York when we passed a panelled wooden fence. He said to me that analysing the spacing and other peculiarities of the fence posts is the model the social scientist might use to understand people in society. He meant that this procedure ignores what matters most in society.

To bring together science and the feeling side of things is the issue faced by the personalities in this part of this book. The great Riverside Church in New York, up by Columbia University, always reminds me of Harry Emerson Fosdick. The great Gothic quadrangles of the University of Chicago remind me of Charles Hartshorne. When visiting Columbia University I think of the lecture room where I got to know Paul Tillich and there is now a street I can walk by Union Theological Seminary called Reinhold Niebuhr place (previously part of 120th Street). Many other philosophers of religion could be added to my list, but I discuss people whose thought I got to know, and whom I know personally as well.

Harry Emerson Fosdick

(Photograph by Lilo Kaskell)

Harry Emerson Fosdick helped me to find my way through fundamentalism to a rational Christian faith. I met him just a couple of times when he was the famed preacher of Riverside Church in New York and professor of homiletics at Union Theological Seminary close by. Most of his influence for me was through his book *Three Meanings: The meaning of faith, the meaning of prayer and the meaning of service* and as well his many books of sermons. They reflect a life that had its ups and downs yet Fosdick found the power to see it through. 'Here I am' Fosdick says:

> talking to you about the secret of spiritual power in general, when all the time what I am really seeing in my imagination's

mind's eye is that young man I was years ago, shot to pieces, done in and shattered in a nervous breakdown, foolishly undertaking too much work and doing it unwisely, all my hopes in ashes and life towering over me, saying, you are finished; you cannot; you are done for. People ask me why in young manhood I wrote *The Meaning of Prayer*. That came out of young manhood's struggle. I definitely needed a second chance and reinforcement to carry on with it. I was sunk unless I could find at least a little of what Paul had in mind when he said I can – 'In Him who strengthens me, I am able for anything' [Fosdick 1961 p 64].

Fosdick's history with the church also appealed to me. In 1918 he became preacher at the First Presbyterian Church in New York. While fundamentalists gathered their forces in the wake of the creation versus evolution Scopes trial, Fosdick preached his famous sermon 'Shall the fundamentalists win?' Presbyterian critics found it objectionable. The quarrel went to the General Assembly of the Presbyterian Church; the moderator demanding the ousting of Fosdick. A compromise prevailed in which the Assembly decided Fosdick could still continue in the pulpit of the First Presbyterian Church provided he became a Presbyterian (Fosdick had been ordained a Baptist). This meant prescribing to the Westminster Confession. He resigned saying that creedal subscription to ancient confessions of faith is a practice dangerous to the welfare of the church and to the integrity of the individual conscience. Many of the members of his devoted congregation wept during his farewell sermon. However, John D Rockefeller Jr offered him the pulpit of the fashionable Park Avenue Baptist Church, which was known as the Fifth Avenue Baptist Church. The name led to the rector of the Episcopal Church of the Heavenly Rest to ask

Fosdick, then the Baptist pastor, why they called their church the Fifth Avenue Church when it was not on Fifth Avenue (at one time it was). Fosdick replied we are as near to Fifth Avenue as you are to Heavenly Rest.

Fosdick at first refused Rockefeller's offer for the pastorate of the Fifth Avenue Baptist Church, saying that he did not want to become known as the pastor of the richest man in the country. Rockefeller answered: 'Do you think that more people will criticise you on account of my wealth than will criticise me on account of your theology?' Fosdick was eventually won over when Rockefeller's congregation agreed to form a new international non-denominational church for him. They sold their Park Avenue Church and together with a hefty sum from Rockefeller they built the great 2500 seat (and 200 overflow) neo-Gothic Riverside Church, above the Hudson River near Columbia University. Its architectural inspiration came from Chartres Cathedral and its iconography includes Albert Einstein and Ralph Waldo Emerson. Fosdick stipulated that his stipend not exceed that of regular pastors. Fosdick became a symbol of the struggle for intellectual freedom and rigour within American Christianity. He wrote the hymn 'God of Grace and God of Glory' for the dedication of Riverside Church in 1931:

Set our feet on lofty places,
Gird our lives that they may be
Armored with all Christ-like graces
In the fight to set men free.
Grant us wisdom, grant us courage,
That we fail not man nor Thee.

Fosdick was important to me in two respects. His writings showed me that the fundamentalist's God was not the only version of the

Christian God. There was a liberal version which I didn't know about. Fundamentalism depicts God as supernatural, almighty, coercive, miracle working and judgmental. It holds the Bible up as literal truth. The liberal view replaces these concepts with a God who is persuasive, never coercive and who works within the bounds of a law-abiding universe as depicted by science. Most importantly it does not depict Jesus as God, but as a man inspired by God. For many of us, as students, the most important of Fosdick's sermons was 'The Divinity of Jesus'. Jesus was first and foremost a real man like other men. He revealed what life in its fullness could be like. So in the first place he leads us to understand what a fully human person is like. He was not God. He was not sent from heaven by God. That is a false metaphor of the world we live in. He prayed to God, which was not a matter of talking to himself. What is highest in human life reveals the nature of God. The divinity of Jesus is an affirmation about human nature. The God who was in Jesus giving hope and love and faith in life is the same God who is in us. You cannot have one God and two kinds of divinity, one for Jesus and one for us! If I were struggling with these ideas right now in the 21st century I would find my theological resources in the writings of contemporary Marcus Borg (eg, 1987 and 1995) whose convictions are remarkably similar to those of Fosdick.

The second importance of Fosdick for me was that from him I first learned how to think of God in relation to the world in a rational way. This he did by contrasting two images derived from science. The first is the image of the watch-maker God typified by Isaac Newton. Newton discovered a law-abiding universe in which the fall of the apple from a tree on Earth is to be understood by the same laws that explain the motion of the planets. To Newton the world was to be conceived as a vast machine which, having been created by God in the first place, now went on its way without God's further involvement. It was like a watch, said William Paley, that runs by itself and just as a watch needs a watch-maker so the universe needs a God to have made it in the first place. Having made the universe there is nothing more for God to do than to make corrections to the watch that may be needed from time to time.

Fosdick contrasted this view of the universe with the evolutionary view of Charles Darwin. Darwin put into the centre of attention the idea of process in the universe, growth development and progressive change. The universe is unfinished and in the process of changing. The cosmos was no longer like a watch with the watch-maker standing aside waiting to make an occasional intervention. Creation was not just an event in the past. It was a continuous process going on now. The effect of this on the idea of God is momentous. If the universe is a completed machine God must be behind it. But if it is in process God must be in it. The notion of periodic or occasional divine intervention of William Paley's Newtonian God implies that if God appears only periodically he disappears periodically. Is the occasional God or the ever-active God the nobler concept? It remained for others such as Charles Hartshorne to think this concept through. Darwin himself was confused about a role for God in evolution though Anglican cleric Charles Kingsley did his best to persuade him that there was an alternative to the interventionist Newtonian God (that God being all that Darwin recognised). So far as we know Darwin's views remained unchanged.

On an island off the coast of Maine Fosdick lived by the sea. He did not know the ocean in its vastness. He had never sailed the tropic seas nor the Arctic and Antarctic seas that wash ice packs. Huge areas of the ocean were unknown to him, but still he knew the ocean. Its waters surround the island on which he lived. He could sit beside it, swim in it, sail over it and watch its storms. It has a near end. So it is with God. God has a near end where love, goodness and truth are revealed in the life of Jesus. This same God continues throughout the universe just as Fosdick's bay is a part of the great ocean beyond. The greater ocean is described by Fosdick as the far end; the part of God we can only touch in our imagination.

Charles Raven

(Courtesy of Charles Birch)

Charles Raven influenced my thinking about the same time as I discovered Fosdick. He was Regius Professor of Divinity in the University of Cambridge, master of Christ's College and at one time vice chancellor of Cambridge University. I had read most of his books on science and religion when I met him in Sydney when he was visiting with other Commonwealth vice chancellors. We managed to persuade him to address students in the Great Hall of the University of Sydney and to meet students afterwards into the small hours of the night. He was bewailing the tragic death of some of his best students in war and the loss of what was to have been their studies on the Alexandrians Clement and his student Origen in the 3rd century. It is amazing how these early theologians insisted that a universe which contains the personal is not be interpreted on a lower scale. This is a strong theme in Raven's Gifford lectures on Science and Religion in 1951–52. Raven was handsome. He had an extraordinarily wide knowledge of the history of science and introduced me to the importance of the Cambridge Platonists of the 17th century and lesser-known English theologians and naturalists who argued that nature was an intelligible system and could not be explained in terms either of random movements of matter in space, such as Thomas Hobbes supposed, or of arbitrary interventions of supernatural agencies. Raven was a liberal Christian scholar who, for the most part, did not receive ecclesiastical preferment, probably because of his liberal theology and, at times, caustic tongue. But for those of us in the Student Christian Movement he was a light shining in the darkness.

Robert Maynard Hutchins

(Photograph by Stephen Lewellyn)

Robert Maynard Hutchins could not be described as a philosopher of religion, but he was influential in primarily such ideas and so he is discussed here. Hutchins was only 30 when he became president at the University of Chicago. He was brilliant, handsome, articulate and a commanding presence. Being the youngest university president in the US he had great public appeal. Hutchins and his university appeared on the front cover of *Time* magazine on 21 November 1949 with his quote 'not a very good university, simply the best there is'. He explained to the *Time* correspondent 'The reason Chicago is as good as it is, is that the faculty is of high quality and they are talking to one another.' I experienced this for myself when I was there in 1946 some five years before Hutchins resigned. I recall vividly an address by Hutchins to the packed cathedral-like Rockefeller Chapel in the university. The subject was 'The administrator'. His very first sentence was 'I am not a very good administrator because I did not have the advantage of hearing this address.' He told students that the purpose of the university was to unsettle their minds. A graduate student told him that in her opinion 99 per cent of the people in the US were abnormal. Hutchins replied that in addition to providing an interesting definition of normality, this suggests that the ordinary difficulties of growing up and becoming human, from which the human race has suffered for a million years, had taken on a clinical character that he could not help but hope was exaggerated.

Hutchins told science departments that they were too concerned with fact-finding and not enough with ideas. He told the undergraduate college that it should scrap textbooks and read the great books. He maintained that the world was bewildered because it had forgotten how to read and think. He attributed much of what was good in his university to the deliberate demise of its football team. He said we are working for a university the football team could be proud of! At the time when Hutchins abolished intercollegiate football at the University of Chicago the football coach is reported as saying that it was all 'very well for President Hutchins who has the physique of Sir Galahad to regard football as unnecessary, but the rest of us need athletics'. Hutchins is reported to have replied that 'it is not recorded of Sir Galahad that his physique was exceptional, but only that his strength was as the strength of ten because his heart was pure'.

Hutchins considered that the whole doctrine that we must adjust ourselves to our environment is radically erroneous. Our mission here is to change the environment, not adjust ourselves to it. Yet the dominant theme in much education is 'Adjust yourself to the world' no longer 'Change the world'. In New York I heard Paul Tillich speak on the same theme very much agreeing with Hutchins' stance. Conformity, he argued, was equated with acceptance of corruption. Yet there was in the world today a trend toward conformity. Instead Tillich proposed a threefold directive: to exercise judgment, offer resistance when necessary and strive to effect a personal and universal transformation. The nonconformist, he warned, must be prepared to risk social ostracism, imprisonment or death – as well as the possibility of being wrong. But in urging nonconformity, he said, he who takes risks and fails can be forgiven. He who never takes risks and never fails is a failure in his whole being. Hutchins took the risk during the legendary Hutchins epoch for the university. He sometimes failed. He sometimes succeeded. He wanted to transform the university and also the world. The time was appropriate because of the nuclear threat of annihilation. He said so in an address entitled 'The Good News of Damnation'. The doctrine of damnation is that it might frighten us into doing what we should be doing anyway. His good news was education for enlightenment, especially through his Great Books Program. He confidently expected to see 15 million Americans studying the great works of the human mind within five years. The rest of he world would follow. I believe he got close to attaining his goal. His speech ended with the possibility that nothing can save us. But with the good news of damnation ringing in our ears we may remember the words of William the Silent: 'It is not necessary to hope in order to undertake, nor to succeed in order to persevere.' Hutchins proclaimed that the pursuit of truth through teaching and research is not an adequate statement of the purpose of the university. The purpose of the university is to produce a moral, intellectual and spiritual revolution throughout the world. Yet the modern university he compared to an encyclopaedia. The encyclopaedia contains many truths. It may contain nothing else. Its unity can be found in its alphabetical arrangement. It has departments running from arts to zoology. But neither the student nor the professors know what is the relation of one departmental truth to another. It can only be held together by a common purpose which depends upon deeply held convictions about the nature of man, the ends of life, the purpose of the state and the order of goods (Hutchins 1946).

Journalist Dixon Wester (1948) visited Tasmania 'that remote Van Dieman's Land of the old geographies' in 1945. There he discovered an ardent disciple of Hutchins in the chancellor, Sir John Morris, of the struggling university.

Sir John yearned to create in that pastoral spot the spiritual climate of the University of Chicago. On getting back to his base in Sydney, Wester saw a newspaper headline 'Polygamy OK for Tasmanian Intelligentsia'. The story reported a speech in which Sir John announced that the university should be concerned with intellect not morals. He added that even if a student had 14 wives the university should not be concerned about his morals. Wester recalled a maxim in one of Hutchins' books: the university is intellectual not moral. Wester was sure he had tracked down the disciple to his master. The irony is that no one had a more profound appreciation than Hutchins, with his evangelical background, of the moral bases of intellectual disciplines.

Hutchins fought for freedom of speech against criticism that his university was a hotbed of communism. He even turned one of its wealthiest opponents into a benefactor. 'Americans must decide' he said 'whether they will no longer tolerate the search for truth ... if they will not, then as a great political scientist has put it, we can blow out the light and fight in the dark. For when the voice of reason is silenced, the rattle of machine guns begins' (McNeill 1991 p 65).

The day on which it became certain that atomic energy could

be harnessed for war and for peace was 2 December, 1942 in the University of Chicago. Professor Enrico Fermi directed the operation of the world's first atomic pile. It was in a squash court of Stagg football field. There was a risk, no doubt very slight, that the university would be blown up if the atomic reaction spread beyond the squash court. The decision to go ahead rested on the shoulders of one man: President Hutchins.

And so it was he who unveiled this simple plaque on wall of the squash court:

On December 2, 1942
Man achieved here
The first self-sustaining chain reaction
And thereby initiated the
Controlled release of nuclear energy

On that December day in 1942 Professor Arthur Compton placed a long-distance call to Professor Conant of the Office of Scientific Research and Development at Harvard: 'The Italian navigator has reached the New World' said Compton to Conant. 'And did he find the natives friendly?' asked Conant. 'Very friendly.'

Charles Hartshorne

Charles & Dorothy Hartshorne, University of Chicago, 1960 (Courtesy of Charles Birch)

Charles Hartshorne was professor of philosophy in the University of Chicago when I first got to know him and his wife Dorothy. He was the foremost scholar in process philosophy at the time. This is the name given to the philosophy of AN Whitehead of Harvard University. Hartshorne had been Whitehead's assistant with the responsibility of instructing Whitehead's students. From Harvard Hartshorne joined the staff of the philosophy department in the University of Chicago. That was in 1928, one year prior to the appointment of Robert Maynard Hutchins as president.

Hartshorne, to some extent, shared the excitement of a campus reeling under its controversial president. Hutchins was attempting to do much that Hartshorne would have approved. He was searching for new ethical and practical ideas to mediate between the ultimate ideas and concrete situations, not only in the university, but in the world. At the same time Hartshorne's department had problems with Hutchins. He was critical of pretty well every department and interfered with some of their programmes. In philosophy he tried to appoint Mortimer Adler to the staff without adequately consulting the staff. Adler was Jewish but had a Thomist philosophy. Adler and Hutchins together ran a Great Books course which seemed to some to have an undue emphasis on Thomist thought. Word spread that the University of Chicago was a former Baptist School where Jewish professors taught Catholic theology to atheist students.

The University of Chicago was a vibrant centre which Hartshorne shared. He tells the story of an encounter with Hutchins in the men's room of the faculty club. A member of the club asked Hartshorne: 'Are you still working on God?' Before he could respond to the question the voice of Hutchins came from behind 'He ought to let God work on him.' Hartshorne agreed.

Hartshorne, was at the University of Chicago, as was I, when it was the world-centre of process thought (pansubjectivism) with most of its process thinkers in the Divinity School. However, this Whiteheadian philosophy was against the grain of the current worldview. I discuss this in detail in Chapters 5 and 6. The University of Chicago in the Hutchins–Hartshorne period had, through its Divinity School, a profound impact on the thinking of many students. I mention just two. One of them John Cobb, Hartshorne described to me as his best student. John Cobb tells the story of his transition from an evangelical Southerner to a Whiteheadian in Chapter 1 of his book *Can Christ become Good News Again?* (Cobb 1991). Another rather similar story is told by Martin Gardner (1973) in the form of a novel about an imaginary Southern evangelical student Peter Fromm who was swept off his feet by a confrontation with the teaching of the Divinity School.

But unlike Cobb's story Fromm's has an unhappy ending. These two stories depict two responses on being confronted with a stark new teaching, yet sharing roots with the old. Martin Gardner had been a student of Hartshorne and amongst his many writings is his essay 'The Strange Case of Robert Maynard Hutchins' (Gardner 1997 pp 509–24).

Hartshorne's understanding of how the world works is very similar to that of AN Whitehead and I make no distinction in what follows. I learned about it from my friendship and reading of Hartshorne and my reading of Whitehead who died in 1947 and whom I never met. Whitehead was initially a mathematician and for 10 years collaborated with Bertrand Russell on *Principia Mathematica*. His philosophical works were written when he was a professor of philosophy at Harvard University. His turning to philosophy may have been influenced by the death of his younger son who was killed in World War I at the age of 18. This was an appalling grief to him and it was only with immense discipline that he was able to go on with his work. Bertrand Russell considered him to have one defect as an administrator, perhaps a calculated one: his unwillingness to answer letters. He justified himself by saying that if he answered letters he would have no time for original work.

Much of Whitehead's writings are difficult, and in places obscure. This is also true of some of Hartshorne's writings. An immediate reward for persisting is periodic phrases that are brilliant and full of meaning and oft quoted. Once when Whitehead was asked why he did not write more clearly he replied surprisingly 'because I do not think more clearly'. This humble confession in his case surely means that the subject is so difficult that it is hard to put it into words no matter how much one tries. Whitehead is admitting that some concepts are so complex that words fail to convey the meaning. He said we may never fully understand, but we can increase our penetration. I recall Hartshorne once saying in relation to a problem about relativity that it was one of the sorrows of his intellectual life that he could not see his way clearly into this region of thought. He is not the only one. The astronomer Shapley gave a talk on relativity and explained that the universe might be 'finite and yet unbounded'. In the question period a lady persisted in attacking the idea as absurd. 'Look here Professor Shapley, you say that even if the universe is finite, it has no boundary. Well suppose I were to go all the way out there nine million light years – is that how large you say the universe may be? – suppose I were to go all the way out there and stick my finger out?' 'Madam' Shapley replied, 'I wish you would.' Back to clear thinking. Whitehead had another maxim applicable to all intellectual enquiry, 'Seek simplicity and mistrust it.' Charles F Kettering, one mistrusting sceptic, has said:

First they tell you, you are wrong, and they can prove it.
Then they tell you you're right but it's not important.
Then they tell you it is important but they've
known it for years.

So be patient! Truth will eventually win out. I was once told that a good way to tell how work was going in the laboratory was to listen to the words being spoken. If you hear the word 'impossible' used as an expletive followed by hearty laughter you know somebody's research plans are coming along nicely.

Back to Hartshorne. There are, I heard Hartshorne once say, three alternative ways of interpreting experience in relation to matter.

1. Matter never experiences, but souls do. This is *dualism*.
2. Matter sometimes experiences (in brains). This is *materialism*.
3. Matter always experiences. This is *pansubjectivism* (see Chapters 5 and 6).

I always felt that Hartshorne's alternatives put ideas about the profound philosophical problem of mind and matter quite succinctly.

In 1960 geneticist Jacques Monod's book *Chance and Necessity* appeared in its first edition in French. It so happened that Charles Hartshorne and I were by coincidence teaching in the University of California, Berkeley, at that time. So I was able to pass on to Charles this important book by Jacques Monod. What delighted him was Monod's insistence on the role of chance in evolution. Hartshorne had already come to the conclusion that Charles Darwin was far too much of a determinist to really believe in what he had discovered, namely the role of chance in the evolutionary process. So here was a Darwin successor in Monod putting the record straight. If chance is real then the universe is not completely determined and God is not omnipotent. Degrees of freedom allow not only chance but choice as well. This concept is critical to process thought.

My most vivid memory of Hartshorne is his presence. He looked at you with an intense interest as though not wanting to miss anything. At that moment you were the most important person in the world for him. And with it came that angelic smile beckoning onwards. His face changed its expression with everything he said and heard. There was always an intense concentration on what was going on in his mind. That made even the briefest encounters such a privilege. He was ever so tolerant and understanding of those who differed from him. His wife Dorothy was less tolerant of the critics. Charles would simply respond 'Oh Dorothy'.

Charles Hartshorne appeared to me to be utterly convinced in his philosophy of life, that I wondered if there was any room for doubt. I had the temerity to ask him if he ever thought that he might be completely wrong. 'It sometimes happens', he replied, 'but not often'. What lies behind his response to my question is that there can be no dogmatic certainty about these propositions. The same holds for science. Charles Hartshorne lived for 103 years. In his 100th year he wrote his last book *The Zero Fallacy*. He died in his sleep on 9 October 2000. Dorothy Hartshorne died some years earlier in a nursing home after she had developed Alzheimer's syndrome. I recall Charles sadly saying to me she had died years before her clinical death. He had been very dependent upon her for her editing of his work. She made an early decision in their marriage to work for Charles' career rather than continue her own work as an editor.

Paul Tillich

I first came to know of theologian Paul Tillich and his ideas by attending his course on Protestantism and Culture at Columbia University. He impressed me as one of the most erudite scholars I had ever known. He had an ability to trace from memory the history of an idea through its main stages of development, observing its subtle shifts in nuances of meaning at the main turning points. He felt himself called to be a teacher with an intense consciousness. He was ever awake to the possibilities of any occasion. He deeply aroused his hearers giving them the feeling that he understood them. This was his appeal to the spoken word. The spoken word is effective not only through the meaning of its sentences, but also through the immediate impact of the personality behind the sentences. Neither Jesus nor John the Baptist said anything really new in their popular preaching. Most of their ideas were already present in the prophets. But they were put with a new force and immediacy. An idea may have been an old one; but in the mind of Tillich it came to life, he was aglow with it. In every lecture he came to the desk with a pile of notes, but he never got beyond the first page. One wondered if he had the whole lecture on the top sheet of paper. He never read but spoke as though he was engaging with each individual student. Henry Sloane Coffin, then president of Union Theological Seminary, sat in on Tillich's first lectures after his escape from Nazi Germany. Coffin later remarked that he did not understand what Tillich said 'but when I look at his face I believe'.

Psychologist Rollo May, who was one of his students, wrote of Tillich's lectures:

> So great was his empathy that he seemed, in his lectures, to have been present when Socrates was forced to drink the hemlock, and when Copernicus demonstrated that the earth moves around the sun, he was there when Luther nailed his 99 theses to the door of the Cathedral. Each of us listeners felt, when Tillich spoke in broken English, that we heard vital truths, many of us for the first time [May 1988 p 116].

Tillich rarely turned a question down. I remember in a response to a question from a student he said 'Only a line and a half but logically and grammatically infinitely difficult'! His strongly accented English added to his charm as a lecturer. He came to the US from Nazi Germany at the age of 47 speaking virtually no English. In his early days of learning English, much to the amusement of the students he referred to Beethoven's 'Moonshine Sonata'. And on being questioned as to whether St Paul didn't get the world out of one mess to plunge it into another, he looked puzzled. 'Vat iz mess?' he asked. The student rephrased the question and substituted the word 'jam'. 'And what iz jam?' Tillich asked.

Tillich's positive attitude to his students reminded me of a quotation I learned from ecologist Professor Evelyn Hutchinson of Yale: 'Never try to discourage a student for you will almost certainly succeed.' In a class I asked Tillich about an issue raised in one of his books. He said in no uncertain terms that what he had written he had written and he had done his best. According to Lucien Price, recorder of dialogues with Whitehead, 'As to touching subject matter, he [Whitehead] had never liked to be quizzed about his published works. There they were, in print, to be read. He had done his best to make them intelligible. Let us go on to something new' (Price 1954 p 19). I see the point.

Tillich said of himself that his whole theological work had been directed to the interpretation of religious symbols in such a way that secular men and women could understand and be moved by them. I give examples later.

My second understanding of Tillich's thought was his sermons, several of which I heard at the James Memorial Chapel of Union Theological Seminary in New York. Many of them were published in books. James Memorial Chapel in those days served as a centre where staff of the seminary became better known to both students and the public.

I had a lunch hour group of students at the University of Sydney who met weekly to discuss Tillich's books. We got so much out of this exercise that we thought Tillich would like to know. So we wrote to him and he replied:

> Your letter is one of the kindest and most encouraging I have ever received. Thanks, many thanks! I am especially happy about the fact that (your group) is not within the 'theological circle', but comes from science and the humanities. It is more and more my conviction that the preservers of the 'vertical', the dimension of depth, are small groups like yours, which concentrate on a book or a problem. There are many of them now springing up in this country also. With my best wishes for your further work. Gratefully yours. Paul Tillich.

The 'dimension of depth' that Tillich refers to in this letter is a critical aspect of what he means by the word religion. Religion is not a special function of man's spiritual life. But it is the dimension of depth in all of its functions. The word depth points to that which is ultimate and unconditional in every aspect of the human spirit, be it science or morality or anything else. But if religion is present in all functions of life why have humans developed religion as a special function in myth, cult, devotion and what is usually called religion? The answer Tillich gives is because of the estrangement of human life from its own depth. According to the visionary who wrote the last book of the Bible there will be no temple in the heavenly Jerusalem, for God will be all in all. There will be no secular realm and for this reason there will be no religious realm. Religion will be the all-determining ground and substance of all life, which gives creative courage to all functions of the human spirit.

This has led me to look for the meaning of depth in physics and biology. It is to imaginatively look beyond our mechanistic models as did physicist David Bohm in his concept of the implicate order and as did biologists WE Agar and CH Waddington in their pursuit of the subjective as when Agar wrote: 'all animals are subjects'.

Why the search for meaning of depth? Human life is estranged from what it could be and from God. Estrangement implies a fundamental belongingness and therefore an inner drive toward reunion. Human beings attempt to find fulfilment in 'idolatries' such as status, sex, nationalism, quasi-religions such as communism or even the church. Against such idolatry Tillich invoked what he called 'ultimate concern'. All these idolatries are lesser concerns.

How sure can we be when we pursue meaning? Tillich said he saw his mission to bring faith to the faithless and doubt to the faithful. Doubt is an inevitable part of faith.

The fundamental question of the Reformation concerned the locus of religious authority. The Protestant Principle is that neither pope nor the church possessed the competence to define Christian belief. There are no institutions nor books that can claim to know the truth. They can point us to paths to truth. Martin Luther claimed that the church was not an authority to be trusted with truth. He then saw the Bible as the source of truth, but quickly realised that the Bible had to be interpreted. He had his own theologian Philip Melanchthon, but other theologians disagreed with his interpretation. Even 2 Peter 3:16 says 'The letters of our brother Paul are difficult to understand.' The daring risk that Protestantism took as its central principle is that there is no authority, neither person, church nor book. There is no authority other than the human conscience which, even so, differs from person to person. Luther taught 'the priesthood of all believers'. The principle is also incorporated in the motto of the Royal Society of London in its founding in 1662 *Nullius in verba* (by the words of no one).

Religion is the state of being grasped by the infinite seriousness of the question of the meaning of our life and our readiness to receive answers. In pursuing that Tillich purged religious thought of literalism and obscurantism and related Christian theology to every discipline. If you eliminate the fraudulent, the sentimental, the illusory and literalism, there is still a hard core in religion. In identifying that hard core Tillich created enemies from amongst the fundamentalists and orthodox and even from some liberal American Protestants who regarded him as a closet supernaturalist. Tillich pleaded that Christians not abandon the Bible to fundamentalists who are notable for their hostility to biblical scholarship. The orthodox rejected Tillich because he was highly suspicious of attempts to fossilise belief in creeds. For the first 300 years of Christianity many possible interpretations of belief were formulated. They were finally reduced by the Council of Nicea in the 4th century to one formula. It was too narrow. The whole history of Christian dogma is a continuous narrowing down into definitions that led to losing the spirit of the enterprise. It is the task of each generation to re-think meaning in the light of cultural advances such as those that come from science. It is like a man riding a bicycle who keeps his equilibrium by constant forward movement. This can be done by formulating revised creeds or as Fosdick chose: to have new understandings but without creeds.

Tillich's colleague and friend Reinhold Niebuhr said of Tillich that he was trying to walk a fence between man's doubts and the traditions of his faith. He walked that fence with great virtuosity and if he slipped a bit to one side or the other it was hardly noticed by us humble pedestrians.

Us humble pedestrians are guided by a light on the hill. It is 'ultimate concern'. I came to see this as central to Tillich's appeal. We have many concerns with each day. It may be concern for food, shelter, entertainment, status and sex. None of these are ultimate in the sense of meeting our sense of estrangement and fulfilling our lives. Like biblical Martha we are concerned about many things, but miss the one thing that matters. That is the concern that is ultimate in the sense of fulfilling human life. This is the pearl of great price. The only appropriate response to ultimate concern is with infinite passion: with all our mind and soul and strength. This was Mary's concern when Jesus visited the home of Mary and Martha. Ultimate concern has the subjective side that is our being ultimately concerned. The objective side is the *object* of our ultimate concern. This object is called God. Tillich would have liked to have called for a moratorium on the word

'God' because of the variety of meanings given to it, and replaced it with 'ultimate concern'. Likewise he avoided the word 'sin'. It had become distorted to mean acts that contradict conventional morality especially in relation to sex. His alternative word for 'sin' is 'estrangement'.

Daniel Day Williams

I was fortunate to know Daniel Day Williams who succeeded Paul Tillich in the chair of philosophy of religion at Union Theological Seminary in New York. I knew him first at the University of Chicago. He was a process theologian and scholar of Whitehead.

He asked directly: 'What does God do in the world?' I used this question in the title of an essay I wrote in the Festschrift in his honour in 1975. He recognised that the greatest difficulty in relating the theological doctrine of God's action to a scientific understanding lies in the problem of assigning specific, observable consequences to divine activity in the world. As a process theologian he looked rather to the nature of the world. Science has its image, which has been strictly mechanistic. It has been highly successful in explaining the external or objective nature of things. Process thought looks at the inner nature of things, which is their subjective nature. The battle to tie the two together is still being fought. In this view God does not affect directly the outward or objective aspects of things, that is the province of modern science, such, for example, as the genetic mutations on which selection acts. God acts directly on the inner aspects of entities from quarks to humans by confronting them with possibilities and values. Whether the entities respond to these possibilities is up to them. Each one has its own degree of freedom to either respond or not. Presumably, the degree of freedom is greatest at the higher levels such as in the case of human beings. The nature of the entity at, say, the level of the electron is presumably much more fixed. The concept of God's involvement in the inner aspect of entities is akin to Tillich's concept of God as the 'ground of being'. Withdraw God and the entity no longer exists. Take away God from the world and the world no longer exists. When God influences the inner aspects of entities their outer aspects change. This perspective of divine activity is vastly different from the view that God directly changes the outer aspects of things, which posits that he can create new species in the twinkling of an eye. Instead God is never coercive, always persuasive. God is not a part-time operator. God's activity is continuous. God's action is not supernatural; it is natural.

Reinhold Niebuhr

The two best-known theologians in the US in the 20th century were Paul Tillich and Reinhold Niebuhr. Both were brilliant and persuasive preachers. My first encounter with Niebuhr's thought was when he was a favourite theologian in Student Christian Movement (SCM) circles in Australia. At the time I, and some of my colleagues, had a negative reaction because we thought he was too ambiguous. Much later Niebuhr told me that the SCM had invited him to visit Australia but he had refused because the programme proposed was far too strenuous; visiting universities in every state. My view of Niebuhr changed when I met him a number of times in New York. And I was very happy to be asked to read the lesson when he came to the University of Chicago to preach in the cathedral-like Rockefeller Chapel. I well remember the occasion because the lesson from Romans 8 commenced with the words 'The whole of creation groaneth and travaileth in pain.' I checked on the pronunciation of that difficult word travaileth and decided on travale-eth. Niebuhr mounted the pulpit to read his text as travel-leth. Maybe I was the only one to be so aware of the difference.

What I came to appreciate was Niebuhr's polemics against the so-called 'social gospel' of the early 20th century, associated particularly with the name Walter Rauschenbusch. Niebuhr regarded the utopian visions of the social gospel as dangerous illusions that prevented the church from responding realistically to a profound moral and political crisis. The urge to live fully, in itself praiseworthy, becomes transmuted by overweening self-interest. It leads to destructive competition for a place in the sun. Niebuhr believed that all moral or social achievements are corrupted by a certain amount of inordinate self-love. Those who do not know the power of self-will have a fatuous and superficial view of human nature. An adequate political ethic is not established merely by conceiving the most ideal possible solution to political problems. It must deal with the realities of human nature as well as ideal possibilities. The task is to establish a tolerable community within the limits set by human recalcitrance. In the real world the search for moral righteousness is filled with ambiguity. The characteristic of the human condition is ambiguity: the inseparable mixture of good and evil, of true and false, creative and destructive forces, both individual and social and the constant tension between the ideal and the actual. We may think we are good and are easily swollen by pride because others think well of us. But we should remember that they do not know the secret of our hearts. Charles Hartshorne had a similar view of human nature recognising that our feelings toward one another are always mixed and the only pure love is God's love. Tillich agrees:

There is a non-Christian in every Christian. There is a weak being in every strong one. There is cowardice in every courage, and unbelief in every faith and hostility in every love [Tillich 1963 p 127].

Niebuhr was emphatic that a civil society prospers best in an atmosphere that encourages neither an overly pessimistic, nor an overly optimistic view of human nature. It recognises how weak are the bonds of morality and decency, which protect a human community from total collapse. This approach became known as Christian Realism. For example 'realism' in foreign policy means not expecting democracy to flourish where it has no roots. Niebuhr practised what he preached in his intense involvement with many social and political movements at the highest level. Christian Realism means the realisation that the destruction of the most tyrannical powers does not guarantee justice. It merely creates the minimal conditions under which the struggle for justice may take place. Under Christian Realism the economic power of the US, for example, must be seen as a special temptation to pride; a hazard to the creation of world community. Yet let us not despair. Niebuhr had a wonderful phrase to express different attitudes to despair: there are those who are not perplexed, those who are perplexed to the point of despair and those who are perplexed, but not to the point of despair. Those who are not perplexed have dissolved all the perplexities of life by some simple scheme of meaning. Christian Realism does not pretend to resolve all perplexities. For Niebuhr it escapes despair by holding fast to what he said is 'the transforming love of God as revealed in Jesus no matter what the circumstances'. He is the author of the *Serenity Prayer* used by Alcoholics Anonymous:

God give us grace to accept with serenity the things that cannot be changed, courage to change the things that should be changed, and the wisdom to distinguish the one from the other.

In 1957 evangelist Billy Graham led a crusade in New York City. Niebuhr opposed its sponsoring by the churches. Even the social gospel of an earlier period was superior to what Niebuhr saw as the pietism of Graham with its high-pressure salesmanship. It gave simple answers to insoluble problems and led to a faith distorted by biblical literalism. It encouraged the belief that good people will be really good and given enough of them they will save the world.

I attended one of Graham's packed meetings in Madison Square Garden in New York. Afterwards I questioned Niebuhr on his views of the crusade. He told me of the case of a youth who responded to the appeal at the end of the meeting to accept Christ and be saved. He confessed a murder in New Jersey recently and asked for forgiveness. The answer to his problem was not that easily solved. Henry van Dusen the president of Niebuhr's seminary made a remark in favour of the crusade, despite his agreement with many of Niebuhr's criticisms. It was that many, of whom he was one, would never have come within the sound of Niebuhr's voice if they had not first been touched by an earlier message from Graham. I myself was initiated into Christianity through fundamentalism, but stayed by virtue of discovering a liberal faith through the Student Christian Movement. We cannot know the truth outright until we are ready to accept it. In the meantime we may have to live with very imperfect symbols and metaphors. They may carry us through until we can accept more substantial symbols of faith.

The importance of Niebuhr's stance on social and political problems really only dawned on me when I was on the working committee of 'Church and Society' of the World Council of Churches (my involvement spanned 20 years). Our job was to provide guidance on social and political issues raised by science and technology. The issues ranged from nuclear power to the limits to growth to molecular biology. We were fortunate that the full-time director of the programme, Paul Abrecht, had been Niebuhr's assistant at Union Theological Seminary in New York. This was his and our opportunity to put Niebuhr into practice and avoid uncritical optimism without being defeatist. The programme was greatly enhanced by Paul Abrecht's ability to persuade top flight scientists to work with the group.

There is an important connection between Reinhold Niebuhr and Paul Tillich. When Tillich was put on Adolf Hitler's list of proscribed professors Niebuhr invited him to come to Union Theological Seminary in New York. Tillich was duly sacked from his post in Frankfurt University and subsequently made his way to New York in 1933. Niebuhr recognised Tillich's brilliance, though they had important differences. Tillich was calling for self-fulfilment. Niebuhr stressed that he who finds his life shall lose it. Tillich stressed the flourishing of the individual life. Niebuhr stressed the social context with all its ambiguities. Whilst Niebuhr was not a contributor to process studies his response to Whitehead and Hartshorne was highly favourable. In his review of Whitehead's *Science and the Modern World* he said Whitehead's philosophy is 'exactly the emphasis which modern religion needs to rescue it from defeat on the one hand and from a too costly philosophical victory on the other' (Brown, James and Reeves 1971 p 22).

I am fortunate to have lived in the golden age of the intellectual preacher; Tillich and Niebuhr are two such classic examples. For a whole year in the University of Chicago in the 1940s I knew that on every Sunday at 11 in the morning the service in the University of Chicago Chapel would have a great preacher from across the US or from around the world. The preacher would always hold court to a packed congregation. The university owes its existence (including the chapel), largely to the benefactions of John D Rockefeller Sr. The students are reputed to sing in the chapel 'Praise God from whom oil blessings flow!'

The age of great preachers is now largely in the past and the 'College Circuit' for them in the US is no longer. What is even more surprising to me is that the Tillich and Niebuhr of the past are no longer known and are little read. Hence the sad remark of Tillich towards the end of his life to theologian Langdon Gilkey 'Vy, Langdon, am I so soon on ze dust-heap of history?' The same could be said of the Student Christian Movement (SCM) throughout the world, which for 100 years stood for a credible alternative to fundamentalism and for which I and many of my colleagues are eternally grateful. The SCM now hardly exists, though it is needed more than ever with the rise of fundamentalism amongst student groups throughout the world.

4 SCIENCE AND RELIGION

A famous astronomer visiting the theologian Karl Barth said to him 'I have a very simple view of religion – do unto others as you would have them do to you.' 'I have,' said Karl Barth, 'a very simple view of astronomy – twinkle twinkle little star, how I wonder what you are.' Such simplistic concepts are caricatures of science and religion. So AN Whitehead (1933 p 229) called for a 'more subtle science and a deeper religion' in order to reconcile the two. Much has already been said on science and religion in previous chapters. Here I try to bring together some of the threads.

There are three major views of the relation between science and religion. The 'conflict thesis' holds that science and religion are inherently, and hence perpetually, in opposition. The only way to overcome the conflict is for one to be obliterated. Richard Dawkins who writes persuasively on the issue, argues that there is no legitimate source of knowledge about the world other than science, certainly not religion. Some Christian fundamentalists hold that it is science that must, at least, be subordinated to their religious views. However as theologian Rudolf Bultmann declares, modern science has made it impossible for anyone to accept the New Testament view of the world. Its account of hell, a three storey universe, spirits and miracles and a mythical eschatology can no longer be accepted by modern humans. These concepts need to be de-mythologised, in so far as that is possible. The main conflict between science and religion is between a materialistic science and a supernatural religion that invokes miracles. Whitehead's 'more subtle science' is one that allows for the subjective as part of reality and Whitehead's deeper religion is one that sees God as persuasive and never as one that intervenes in the natural world.

A second view of the relation between science and religion is the 'contrast thesis'. It holds that science and religion are so different that they ask different questions. For example, they claim that science answers 'how questions' and religion deals with 'why questions'; a concept I discuss below.

A third position is the 'integration thesis'. Science and religion can be integrated into a self-consistent worldview. But this can only be done if the common understanding of science becomes more subtle and that of religion becomes deeper. A role of science is to winnow out the superstitious and dross from religion. Science raises critical questions with regard to any kind of belief in God. Belief in God raises critical questions with regard to any kind of science.

This book seeks to promote the integration thesis. As a result of the dialogue between scientists and theologians there have indeed been changes in understanding. But at the same time both wider communities have failed to keep pace with these parallel changes. New understandings struggle to gain a hearing in either community. What emanates from pulpits is more likely to represent the conflict thesis or the contrast thesis.

Three contesting views

In the following historical account I have been very much dependent upon David Griffin (2000). At the time of the Reformation and the Renaissance of science the church had before it three alternative worldviews. There was the scientific doctrine of *mechanism* or materialism derived from Isaac Newton and Galileo Galilei. There was the *Aristotelian* authority of the Scholastics. Thirdly there was an *organic* lesser-known view espoused by people such as Paracelsus, John Dee and Giordano Bruno.

It is an extraordinary fact of history that not only science but also Western Christianity accepted the doctrine of the mechanistic universe. The universe was a clockwork. God was the clock maker. Churches began to put clocks in their towers to instruct the faithful in the way of the creator. Clocks were more than time-keepers. They were homiletic devices. But as David Hume pointed out the God whom you will find in a mechanical universe will be the sort of God who makes machinery, in other words a mechanic. The French priest Marin Mersenne, who was René Descartes' chief correspondent on these matters, hoped to replace 'The Imitation of Christ' by 'The Imitation of the Divine Engineer'. In our day the 'mind' of God becomes, for physicist Stephen Hawking, the ultimate mathematical equation that purports to explain 'everything'.

The clockwork world and the clockmaker God were taken over by the Protestant Reformers in the 16th century. While Martin Luther's view of the universe as mechanism contains ambiguities, John Calvin who followed, had a strictly mechanistic view. History was simply the unwinding of the clock that God wound up at the beginning.

The neglected third alternative – the organic view of the universe, in which God and mind were part and parcel of ongoing nature – was rejected, though it had more elements than mechanism that were congenial to a religious position. There were many reasons for this rejection including its magical elements.

Four consequences of the view of the God of mechanism are:

- It had no answer to the mind-body problem.
- It had no answer to the problem of evil.
- Science found it had no need of God in its explanations.
- Theology found it had no need of science in its explanations.

The God of mechanistic science retreats with the advance of science (as Galileo thought and as Darwin showed). The gaps that God had occupied were filled by science. God was pushed back first to the origin of life and then to the origin of the universe.

Theology found it had no need of science. The church divided the world into two different realms: one material (which was the province of science) and the other spiritual (which was the province of theology). It was a tragic cutting up of a seamless robe. False dichotomies arose. Science was concerned with 'how'; religion with 'why'. Science dealt with 'what is' and religion with 'what ought to be'. Any religion worth its salt should be concerned with the nature of what is, as well as why it is. Science asks 'why' questions as well as 'how' questions. It is a scientific question to ask: 'Why is it that cicadas have reproductive cycles that are 13 or 17 years long but never 15 or 16?' Likewise it is perfectly legitimate for a scientist to ask: 'Why do birds sing?' Good science is also concerned with 'ought' questions. Why else would Robert Oppenheimer have said after the dropping of the atomic bomb on Japan: 'We scientists ourselves have known sin.' He was recognising the social responsibility of scientists who have so dramatically changed our world in the past few decades.

The mechanistic worldview was at first theistic and dualistic. God and nature were separate as were mind and matter. This is deism, which is a compromise between supernaturalism and naturalistic science. God, after creating the world, no longer acts in it. It is a half-way house to atheism. Hence in its second phase the mechanistic worldview was atheistic and materialistic, which is the dominant position today.

What science has done to religion is to debunk the argument for God as the designer of nature and omnipotent supernatural power of the universe. Science has no place for the interventionist God. That is good. There is another view. God's power is not the power to do anything at all, to manipulate things and people. It is the power of persuasive love working in a world of entities endowed with a degree of self-determination. The entities can either respond or not respond. All chapters of this book have something to say about science and religion and elaborate on this brief account.

Of the four people who represent science and religion below, Ian Barbour and John Habgood are still alive. Many others have made their mark in this debate; too many to list. Furthermore, much of this subject is discussed under the names above such as Dobzhansky and Hartshorne (hence the brevity of this section).

Carl von Weizsäcker

(Photograph by Ian Howard)

Carl Friedrich von Weizsäcker is a German physicist and philosopher, son of Ernst von Weizsäcker senior official in the Ministry of Foreign Affairs under Adolf Hitler, and brother of Ernst who became president of the Federal Republic of Germany in 1985. Carl von Weizsäcker had shown that, at the high temperatures inside stars, energy liberated from the nuclear fusion of hydrogen to form helium could supply stellar luminosity. He, together with Werner Heisenberg, was commissioned by Adolf Hitler to initiate the German 'uranium project' to construct an atomic bomb.

I visited him in June 1969 when he was professor of philosophy and rector of Hamburg University. I was representing a small group of biologists in the USA and the UK who were concerned about the grave ethical and philosophical problems of modern biology. American geneticist Michael Lerner said to me he could see no guide from science, philosophy, religion or sociology, as they existed today and time was running out. The physicists had already been through the birth pangs of the atomic age. James Watson, who won the Nobel Prize with Francis Crick for the discovery of the double-helix structure of DNA wrote in an essay in *Time* magazine claiming that in 1948 biology was near the bottom of science's totem pole with physics at the top. But today, he said, molecular biologists are both revered and feared, just as nuclear physicists were in the 1940s.

My mission to Hamburg was to ask Weizsäcker if he would be willing to participate in a project on ethical issues in modern biology. His initial comment was that we must not let ourselves be overcome by biology, as was the case with physics. He was unable to join our group, but gave me the names of some German biologists who were already involved. Weizsäcker was a physicist who recognised something many biologists fail to see, and that is the distinction between the objective account of science and the subjective. A huge gap exists between what science tells us and what we experience. For example, biologists study the biological correlates of consciousness, but ignore the subjective aspect. Suppose I am speaking to an audience. What is speech? Nothing but sound waves you say. But these sound waves carry a meaning which some of my hearers understand. They have come to the lecture, not for the sound waves, but for the meaning they carry. This example from Weizsäcker makes the distinction between the objective and the subjective very clearly. It carries over into his understanding of the relation between science and religion.

An outcome of my discussion with Weizsäcker was a series of symposia over many years under the auspices of the World Council of Churches (WCC). The WCC was already committed to a programme on the future of humanity in a world of science and technology. This is not the place to summarise the results of these programmes, which were mostly in the fields of atomic energy, conservation, genetics and molecular biology. In the broadest terms biology has put into our hands the means of controlling our own destiny through negative eugenics, positive eugenics, genetic engineering, molecular therapy, genetic counselling, foetal diagnosis, selective abortion, behaviour control and other issues. Our response to the questions raised depends upon what we think the human is and what constitutes quality of life and its fulfilment. So those involved in our discussion were not only biologists but included philosophers, ethicists and theologians. One quickly got to know which biologists were in a specialist groove and which, such as geneticist Theodosius Dobzhansky, were alert to the wider implications of their science.

Margaret Mead

(Photograph by Lotte Jacobi)

With her big stick and commanding presence Margaret Mead always stole the show. She stood high in the World Council of Churches certainly with those of us with a scientific background. It was because of her that the WCC developed a programme on science and technology in relation to the future of humanity. At the fourth Assembly of the WCC in Uppsala in 1968 Margaret Mead dramatically convinced the assembled company that it was absurd for the WCC not to have a programme on the huge impact of science and technology on society. The division of Church and Society was given the responsibility of carrying out the programme. The first stage was an exploratory conference in Geneva in 1970 that brought together scientists, theologians and church leaders. The conference was surprisingly successful despite the fear that it would detract from the WCC emphasis on social justice. In fact the opposite was the case. Margaret Mead played a key role. What really surprised me was her evangelical zeal. For example, at the height of the conference she called upon anyone so moved to stand up and make a statement of faith. Many did.

The next step was to create a working committee to develop plans for the inquiry for the next few years. It met in the beautiful village of Nemi overlooking a crater lake in the Alban Hills south of Rome. Margaret Mead was an important member of the on-going committee. She was particularly enthusiastic about the contingent of young people whom director Paul Abrecht had recruited for the meeting. One of them was Jurgen Randers, a co-author of *The Limits to Growth* to be published in 1972. He gave us a preview together with striking graphs of resource and population overshoot. We knew that this had to be on the programme. Indeed it became central in a meeting at Bucharest in 1974, at which the phrase 'ecological sustainability' was coined. It quickly spread around the world. Randers and I were conducting a workshop on limits to growth. The workshop was not getting anywhere with third world delegates saying 'Don't talk to us about limits to growth. What we need is to grow as the rich nations have grown.' At a coffee break Randers said to me that we had to find some phrase other than limits to growth that was positive in its impact. He made a number of suggestions and then said: 'What about the ecologically sustainable society?' When we put this to the workshop they all said of course we want an ecologically sustainable society. The concept was accepted by the full conference and sped around the world like wildfire. It was incorporated into the next seven-year programme of the WCC under the title of 'The Just Participatory and Sustainable Society'. Margaret Mead played a critical part in promoting the programme. I recall vividly waiting with her for a taxi outside our hotel in Bucharest when several Mercedes pulled up to collect government ministers of the then communist government in Romania. I remarked on what I thought was an inconsistency in such a display of wealth by the top echelons. Margaret simply replied: 'Nothing but the best for the people and their representatives!' Some people expressed surprise that Margaret was so involved in a church-sponsored activity. She was an Episcopalian. And at times she led the worship activities at conferences. It was characteristic that she would complain about the formal seating of row behind row and where possible called upon those gathered to form a circle. One of her great insights was: 'Never doubt what a small group of thoughtful committee citizens can do to change the world.' 'Indeed,' she said, 'it is the only thing that ever has.' That is the sort of encouragement individuals and committees need. Another of her much quoted statements is 'Always remember that you are absolutely unique. Just like everyone else.'

Fifty-five years ago Margaret Mead said that the central problem agitating young people was *identity*. Thirty-five years ago she said the central problem of young people was *commitment*.

This she said in the Wayside Chapel in Kings Cross, Sydney. Her friends were a bit reluctant when they learned that I had asked her to address question time in the chapel theatre on a Sunday evening. Their concern was that the meeting could get rough for it was well known that it attracted social dropouts, prostitutes, drug addicts, the lost and some who were verbally aggressive. When I explained this to her she wavered not an iota. The full theatre listened with rapt attention. They respected the genuine and committed. Their questions were thoughtful and sincere. They needed the *commitment* she spoke about.

I now wonder what word she would have chosen as representing a characteristic need of today's youth. When I put this question to a friend who is much involved with youth today he immediately answered: 'Meaning.' 'To be or not to be' was Hamlet's question. To find an answer to the meaning of life was his quest. It is Paul Tillich's 'ultimate concern'. If homes, schools, universities and churches do not communicate a meaning of life then lesser concerns take over and ultimately emptiness prevails. A life that does not take anything with ultimate seriousness is not worth living. Very soon the demonic takes the place of emptiness, as happened under Nazism. According to psychiatrist Viktor Frankl some 20 per cent of neuroses are due to what he calls an existential vacuum resulting from lack of any meaning in life. He identifies a *will to meaning* in contrast to Jeremy Adler's *will to power* and Sigmund Freud's *will to pleasure*. People do not care so much for pleasure and avoidance of pain, says Frankl (1959), but they do care for meaning. Being human is pointing beyond oneself and being directed to something or someone other than self.

Five years after Margaret Mead's death the Australian anthropologist Derek Freeman attacked Mead's anthropology, both her methods and her conclusions. Many defended Mead and many joined with Freeman in his criticism. The issue was one of nature and nurture or what is now known as sociobiology. Biologists are as divided now, as they were earlier, on the relative importance of heredity and environment. Freeman visited me at the height of the controversy, assuming I think, that as a biologist I would be on the side of the sociobiologists. I wasn't. The Freeman attack on Mead was of sufficient public interest to cause the *New York Times* to have it headlined on its front page and to cause the Australian playwright David Williamson to write a play *Heretic* on the subject, which was a success, certainly in Australia.

John Habgood

John Habgood (now Lord Habgood) was Archbishop of York when he became the chairman of our WCC Committee on Science and the Future. He combined both science and theology in his career, having trained first as a physiologist in Cambridge before turning to theology. He was the best chairman of meetings I have experienced. He impressed me as a tolerant churchman, an attitude I appreciated as he was strictly orthodox though broadly liberal at the same time. He was the intellect of the Church of England and should have become the Archbishop of Canterbury. The only time he referred to my own religious stance, so influenced by Whitehead and Hartshorne, was when he said that the trouble with me was that theologically I was 'not trinitarian enough'. I was so puzzled that I did not ask him to elaborate. It seemed to me that there could hardly be degrees of trinitarianism. You either are a trinitarian or you are not. Recently I had the opportunity of reminding Habgood of what he had said about trinitarianism. He responded that he could not imagine saying that. Perhaps he had changed his mind. There was another point of puzzlement between us. A young American theologian Jay McDaniel and I were given the responsibility of a conference on Liberating Life. Its purpose was to discuss the Christian responsibility to non-human creation; an area largely neglected by the WCC because of priority given to social justice and liberation from human oppression. The theme of liberation must be extended to include the Earth and all living creatures. The fact that we were having a conference on this subject under the auspices of the WCC was itself a bit of a triumph. The conference prepared a report, which had a lot to say about animal liberation. After presenting the report to Habgood he was very critical and did not want to pass it on to higher quarters in the WCC. One reason he gave was that he thought it was badly written. But there also seemed to be another hidden reason and that probably had to do with the bad light in which animal liberation was held in England. Extremists had wrecked laboratories and threatened some biologists who worked with animals such as monkeys, cats, dogs and rats. The last thing these scientists needed was an archbishop supporting animal liberation.

That probably coloured Habgood's response to our efforts. He said to me: 'I suppose you will next want to ban horse racing.' 'What a good idea,' I said. However, all ended well with our publishing a book called *Liberating Life*, which contained a chapter by Habgood as well as our report.

Why did Habgood turn from a promising career in science to theology? One reason was what he described as his inability to answer the question: 'Why spend a life doing scientific research?' The only answer he could give then, and the answer given by all his colleagues, to whom he put the question, was 'curiosity'. And that did not, for him, seem to be enough. Lower down the scale of motives for scientists were ambition, economic exploitation, the PhD industry and the publications' race. Had Habgood put his question to me I would have rated above curiosity a socially responsible science that had as its goal increasing the quality of life on Earth. My first job as a scientist was at the Waite Agricultural Research Institute in Adelaide. The institution by its name set the agenda. It was to promote better agriculture. My mentor at the time, HG Andrewartha, worked on projects of practical importance, but in such a way as to add to basic understanding in biology. We worked on a plague grasshopper and I believe we not only helped farmers to make better choices but we added to a basic understanding of the physiology and ecology of insects and the causes of plagues. Later we turned our attention to how to safely store huge quantities of wheat accumulated in Australia during World War II such that they would not be destroyed by insects. To get an answer we had to discover a lot about the metabolism of both wheat and insects and how that caused wheat to heat up and be damaged. The social responsibility of scientists is now recognised in a way that hardly existed 50 years ago.

Ian Barbour

(Courtesy of Ian Barbour)

For 50 years Ian Barbour has been a leader in thinking on the relations of science and religion; culminating in his Gifford lectures in 1989–91. Barbour was professor of Science Technology and Society at Carleton College, Northfield, Minnesota. I knew him first when we were both at the University of Chicago in 1946. He was then studying for a PhD in physics. We both lived in International House, were involved in the Rockefeller Chapel group convened by the dean of the chapel Dean Gilkey and were brought together by our common interest in science and religion. Ian went on to study theology at Yale. I went back to Australia to teach and do research in biology. Ian ended up in a position in science and religion at Carleton College Minnesota. We have been together many times since at meetings and conferences. His many books on science and religion are important, not only because they cover such an enormous field, but because they see process thought as providing the most credible framework for bringing together ideas in science, philosophy and theology (Barbour 1990). He deals with criticisms of process thought in a disarming way. He presents an interpretation of Christianity that is responsive both to the historical tradition and contemporary science.

5 MY PHILOSOPHY OF LIFE: PANSUBJECTIVISM

Ideas about a worldview profoundly shape our lives. 'As we think, we live,' said AN Whitehead (1938 p 63). Deep within us is an image or picture of reality, whether consciously articulated or not, which more than anything else shapes how we live. John Maynard Keynes in *The General Theory of Employment, Interest and Money* (1936) said that ideas are more powerful than is generally understood. Indeed, he added, the world is ruled by little else. The power of vested interests, he believed, is vastly exaggerated compared with the gradual encroachment of ideas.

Ideas are both powerfully creative and destructive. The ancient prophets of Israel warned that some ideas could be destructive if they continued to be acted upon. They pointed to ideas that were transformative. Their purpose was not to reveal the future, but to change it. The stakes were high. The prophet Jeremiah died fleeing to Egypt from Jerusalem. Socrates was executed. So was Jesus. As was Paul. So were Hugh Latimer, Nicholas Ridley, Thomas Cranmer, Michael Servetus and Jan Hus. Their ideas were explosive. Many are called but few are chosen, because apathy so often removes the fuse from explosive ideas.

My ideas have changed. I was brought up as a low-church Anglican in the city of Melbourne. Sin, saving souls, a literal interpretation of the Bible, miracles and the efficacy of the sacrament of communion, were parts of a total package of fundamentalism which I accepted. But rough passages came during adolescence. I believed that I was just not good enough. Even such righteousness as I might have possessed, I was reminded, was 'but as filthy rags'. I believed that I must be very sinful. I read the *Confessions* of Saint Augustine and said to myself: 'that is me'. My self-diagnosis was supported by a fundamentalist group called the Crusaders at my school. I never felt really at home in that group. Indeed I was quite embarrassed. I didn't want to confess my sins, whatever they were, in public and I did not feel comfortable with so-called 'personal testimonies'. I did not know what it meant to give my life to Jesus, which they pleaded me to do. How could I give myself to someone who lived 2000 years ago whom I had never met? 'Be willing to break the ice,' I remember being told. I think it meant that I was to try to get over the first obstacle on the path to conversion and the rest would follow on down the track. Into the long hours of the night I pondered on all this. I felt that life was a great burden and I was unworthy. I found a picture in my copy of *Pilgrim's Progress* of Christian travelling on his long journey with a huge bundle on his back. After many trials and tribulations he reached the foot of the cross. Behold the bundle fell off his back to the ground! That was decisive. I wanted that to happen to me. It did. I remember the time and place. Why do I feel burdened with a load on my back when Jesus said your sins are forgiven? That surely means that the past is the past and I could begin again right now with a clean slate. I prayed for the burden to drop away. It did. I considered myself saved.

I was then an undergraduate at the University of Melbourne, convinced that I had the answer to life's meaning. For four undergraduate years this was my position. In one part of my brain science took control. In another part was religion. The only relation I had between them was that science would eventually get me a job that would enable me to save the world. My faith was firm and my direction fixed.

Things changed when I became a graduate student at the University of Adelaide in its premier agricultural research institute. My colleagues appeared to be either atheists or agnostics. That I took religion seriously seemed strange to them. Dr HG Andrewartha, my supervisor, had thought it all through and had come to the conclusion that religion was anti-science and a source of much evil in society. I had many discussions with him, especially when we went into desert country on field trips. I was quite unable to defend my position intellectually. It was full of holes. Had I known at the time I might have been encouraged by Charles Darwin's similar dilemma. As a student in Cambridge he did not in the least doubt the literal truth of every word in the Bible. Even during the voyage of the *Beagle* he amused the officers with his naïve orthodoxy. He was deeply shocked when one of his shipmates expressed doubts about the biblical account of the flood. His fundamentalist beliefs could not be reconciled with speculations about the origin of species. For a while he fought a rearguard action against his doubts. But in the months following his return from the voyage his new scientific theory was born and his faith in religion was dead.

As for me there came a second conversion. It was an intellectual one. The seeds of doubt had been sown and I desperately wanted to know how to deal with them. My faith, which had given me a tremendous sense of meaning in life, was falling apart. The beginning of a resolution to my pressing search for meaning came through the Student Christian Movement in the University of

Adelaide. It showed me there was an alternative interpretation of Christianity to fundamentalism. When reassurance began to re-establish itself it came like the weaving together of strands. I was conscious of a bottom forming under me. I tried to break it down. The strands refused to be broken. The effect was to re-establish a fundamental trust with respect to the meaningfulness of human life. I found some of the former elements came back, different from the old, no longer borrowed at second hand. For better or for worse, they were mine. A new door opened up in my life.

Elements of my first emotional conversion came back. Renewed were the experience of forgiveness, the courage to face the new, the sense of not being alone in the universe, and all that could be called the values of existence as revealed in the life of Jesus. The experience of God as a source of values was real. My interpretation was different. My new understanding came by degrees.

I had a new problem now. The science I was becoming familiar with presented me with a mechanistic universe, which provided no clues to the meaning of life's fundamental experiences of value. It had nothing to say about feelings, which to me were the most important part of life. How did they fit into a mechanical universe? I started on a new journey of discovery, the story of which comes later in this chapter.

Three worldviews

The context of this story is three contemporary worldviews that have been identified by David Griffin (1989) as the 'modern worldview', the 'deconstructive postmodern worldview' and the 'constructive postmodern worldview'. My evolution is from the 'modern worldview' to the 'constructive postmodern worldview'.

Modern worldview

The 'modern worldview' is also known as the 'mechanistic', 'physicalist' or 'materialist' view. It developed out of the 17th century science of Galileo Galilei, René Descartes, Francis Bacon and Isaac Newton. The 'modern worldview' has become the dominant model over the past 300 years. The machine is the metaphor of the world, not only the living such as the human. Hence Arthur Schopenhauer described the philosopher of materialism as 'the philosopher of the subject who forgets to take account of himself'. The procedure of mechanism is to subdivide the world into its smallest parts, which at one time were thought to be atoms. The essence of atomism is that these parts remain unchanged no matter what particular whole they constitute, be it a star or a human being. Having divided the world into its smallest bits you then try to build it up from the bits and of course what you get is a machine. The principle of mechanism is to interpret the higher (human beings) in terms of the lower (classical atoms); this process is called 'reductionism'. The world so conceived consists of collections of mindless, meaningless, self-contained building blocks not influenced in their nature by anything in their environment. They are like bricks that remain unchanged whether assembled into a factory or a cathedral. The parts themselves are independent. They do not need relationships to other parts for their own existence. This is called a 'substance view' of the world. A 'substance' was defined by René Descartes, as a thing that requires nothing but itself in order to exist. It is a declaration of *independence* of the building blocks of the world. It is a non-ecological view of reality. This is not the case with organisms. The relations of the parts to other parts are essential to what they are. In process thought, actual entities – from quarks to humans – are more like organisms than machines. This is a view that Whitehead came to from two sources: modern physics and evolutionary biology.

By the end of the third decade of the 20th century virtually every main postulate of this classical physics had been controverted, that is to say:

> The atoms as solid, indestructible, and separate building blocks of nature, space and time as independent absolutes, the strict mechanistic causality of all phenomena, the possibility of objective observation of nature [Tarnas 1991 p 356].

By contrast with classical physics, in quantum physics the so-called material world no longer appears as a machine or collection of machines. The downfall of classical physics and the rise of quantum theory refutes physicalism. The world appears more like a network or web of relationships that includes the human observer. Physicist John A Wheeler caught something of this idea when, with his tongue somewhat in his cheek, he declared to his graduate students that he had just discovered that there was only one electron! There must have been some seriousness in his remark because Wheeler was reported as saying to the equally distinguished physicist Richard Feynman, 'Feynman I know why all electrons have the same charge and same mass.' 'Why?' asked Feynman. 'Because they are all of the same electron,' replied Wheeler.

Mechanism has been highly successful as a methodology in the hands of scientists in interpreting the outer aspect of things that can be weighed and measured. It tends to ignore or reject all understanding of the ways of the universe that fall outside its abstractions. Science as now practised is a limited venture concerned with the external and statistical aspects of events. The riddle of the universe is not so simply dealt with as I hope to show. The so-called modern worldview is the conventional wisdom of our time and culture. It is an incomplete view of reality. It is important to appreciate that the material mode of description is that part of a complete mode which is capable of scientific precision. According to Hartshorne (1962 p 217):

> Methodological materialism, or the restriction of attention to this mode, is a natural bias among scientists. Much depends on seeing what I call the complete mode – that is an ultimate idealism or psychicalism – does not preclude any scientific procedure, but merely opens our eyes to the beyond that tends to escape any save a vague, intuitive apprehension.

For example, the current investigations of consciousness by biologists have been successful in identifying what can be called the 'biological correlates of consciousness', but have left untouched its inner aspects or experience. There is a huge gap between what science describes and what we experience. (For example, an electrical current in a nerve cell when we have pain is not itself the feeling of pain.) For the materialist the world is like a complex machine without any inner aspects just as a washing machine has no inner aspects. Some will add a vague belief that the machine was made by God who then left it to run by itself (deism). The early modern worldview (Newton) was dualist and supernaturalist. It evolved to become materialistic (TH Huxley) and atheistic (some Darwinians such as Richard Dawkins). Charles Darwin was a deist. Albert Einstein sometimes spoke as if he were a deist. He is probably best described as a pantheist ('I believe in Spinoza's God').

Bertrand Russell was a materialist, yet he had a strong social conscience. He deplored the effect of materialism on those people who see themselves as cogs in machinery. He even composed a creed for them:

Almighty and most merciful machine, we have erred and strayed from thy ways like lost screws; we have put in those nuts which we should not to have put in, and we have left out those nuts which we ought to have put in and there is no coginess in us [Russell 1968 pp 57–8].

Deconstructive postmodern worldview

The 'deconstructive postmodern worldview' deconstructs or eliminates ingredients such as self, purpose, meaning, value, God, a real world and truth as it is understood in the modern worldview. It leads to relativism and also to nihilism. It is inspired by Martin Heidegger, Jacques Derrida, Gilles Deleuze and other French thinkers. The above statement is very much dependent upon David Griffin's (1989) critique. This view includes some positive philosophical concepts (Keller and Daniell 2002), even though, on the whole, metaphysics tends to be deconstructed to the point of extinction.

Much of the writing of this group is obscure. So irksome is this to some scientists that physicist Alan Sokal made a brilliant hoax by submitting to the US journal *Social Text* in 1996 a paper with a senseless title and which from start to finish was deliberate nonsense crafted in the style of 'metatwaddle'. The paper was accepted for publication after which Sokal revealed that it was a hoax. A brilliant analysis of obscure writing by deconstructive postmodernists can be found in the book *Intellectual Postures* by Sokal and Bricmont (1998). I wish all students who incline to obscurity in writing would read it.

Constructive postmodern worldview

The 'constructive postmodern worldview' challenges both the modern worldview and the deconstructive postmodern worldview. It is the subject of this chapter and Chapter 6. It does not reject science as such, but scientism, in which the data of science alone is allowed to contribute to a worldview. The constructive postmodern worldview seeks a unity of science, ethics, aesthetics and religion. It transcends individualism, mechanism, economism, consumerism, sexism, nationalism, anthropocentrism and militarism. It has to do with our ultimate concern, the meaning of life, and with all the forces that threaten or support that meaning, in personal and social life, in the arts and sciences, in politics, in industry and in education.

The constructive postmodern worldview which this book advocates has a variety of names: process thought, panpsychism (*pan* is Greek for all and *psyche* is Greek for mind: Hartshorne), panexperientialism (Griffin), and pansubjectivism (Cobb). Its theistic version is panentheism (all in God). What follows is my understanding, its meaning to me. Mine is a personal account that does not claim to give the whole of what its exponents such as AN Whitehead or Charles Hartshorne have to say. There are aspects that I find difficult to understand, and some, though understandable, are difficult to explain.

A critical divide exists between pansubjectivism and the modern worldview. It was captured by Bertrand Russell when he said, 'either life is matter-like or matter is life-like'. His belief that life is matter-like, made Russell a mechanist. AN Whitehead argued that matter is life-like, so he was a pansubjectivist.

Instead of regarding material things such as the solid atoms of classical physics as a basis for a concept of nature, Whitehead changed radically this approach. He looked, not to classical atoms but to the living organism for clues. There are good reasons for this. The only entity we know with intimacy is ourself. We have an outsider's view of atoms. We do not know what it is like to be an atom, but only what it is like to be someone doings things with atoms. It is then logical to look to human life to furnish a model of reality rather than to 'mere matter'. There is more to living organisms than collections of classical atoms and molecules. Living organisms are characterised by mentality, self-determination, creativity, purpose. If we ask what the nature of the 'more than materialism' is, it is no extra substance, entelechy or life-force. It is the capacity for feeling akin to unconscious feeling we attribute to ourselves. There is no dividing line between the non-living and the living. All are of a piece.

JS Haldane (father of JBS) argued that a meeting place between biology and the physical sciences will one day be found. If then one of the two sciences is swallowed up, that one will not be biology. The most characteristic feature of living organisms, as distinct from pieces of non-living matter is that they experience or have feelings. Experience becomes the key. Hence Whitehead called the thesis he developed from this the theory of organism (as opposed to strict mechanism). Irreducible brute matter or material in the classical picture is senseless, valueless and purposeless. Organisms have senses, mental attributes, a sense of value and purposiveness. This concept gives a new interpretation of the famous dictum of the Sophist, Protagoras, about the middle of the 5th century BCE 'Man is the measure of *all* things.' Which we could read as 'human experience is the measure of *all* things'. We shall never know Alfred Tennyson's 'flower on the crannied wall' until 'we know what God and man is'. The flower on a crannied wall consists of more than classical atoms and molecules and participates in something of what a human is.

It was this radical realisation that led the 'Romantic Reaction' against mechanism by the poets John Milton, William Wordsworth and Alfred Tennyson. Their characteristic thought opposed to the modern worldview is summed up by Wordsworth's phrase 'We murder to dissect.' Analysis reveals the components, but it disintegrates their relationship to the whole. The romantic reaction was a protest on behalf of value and its exclusion from what we have called the modern worldview. It is the fascinating subject of Chapter 5 in Whitehead's *Science and the Modern World*.

The central concept of pansubjectivism is radical and in some ways shattering to our common-sense point of view. It contends that our individual *experience* as human subjects provides the clue to the nature of *all* individual entities. Experience is the subjective element. Or to put it in another way, all entities from humans down to quarks are seen as centres of experience and not simply objects of experience for others. This we know best in ourselves. The entities of nature from quarks to humans are thought of as belonging to the same category of existence as human experience. These ultimate entities that constitute reality are not to be thought of as substances, such as classical atoms, but as occasions of experience. It is helpful to visualise experience as momentary occasions rapidly succeeding one another. We are aware of this in our own experience which moves quickly from one moment to the next in what is a succession of experiences.

Science finds its facts from the study of the objective aspects of nature. As Whitehead has emphasised, science can find no individual enjoyment in nature, no aim in nature, no creativity in nature (Whitehead 1938 p 154). This is because science deals with only half the evidence provided by human experience. Whitehead follows the above with a statement that science divides the seamless coat or to use another metaphor, it examines the coat and neglects the body. The body has to do with the subjective that is not amenable to weighing and measuring.

But is it not highly anthropomorphic to take human experience instead of things as the model of reality? That depends on what we mean by human experience. If it is thought to be fully embraced by what the five senses tell us we have not advanced upon the modern worldview. If it includes such perceptions as purpose and sense of value, as in process thought, then we are on the track of something tremendously important, indeed so important that Socrates made this a central element in his reminiscences, recorded in the *Phaedo*, as he sat in prison awaiting his death in 399 BCE. Why, he reminisces, was he sitting alone in prison? The scientist Anaxagoras would say:

I am sitting here now because my body is composed of bones and muscles, and that the bones are hard and divided by joints, while the muscles can be tightened and relaxed and, together with the flesh and the skin which contains it, cover the bones; and that therefore when the bones are raised in their sockets by the contraction or relaxation of the muscles I am able to bend my limbs; and that is the cause of my sitting here in prison all huddled up ... I am inclined to think that these muscles and bones of mine would long ago have been in Megara or Boeotia prompted by their own opinion of what is best, if I had not thought it better and nobler to submit to any penalty the state inflicts rather than run away. To call these other things causes is too absurd. Had the contention been merely that without the aid of bones and muscles and the rest I could not carry my purposes into effect, that would have been true enough. But to say that I do what I do because of them and not because my mind knows what is best is a very loose way and careless way of thinking.

The two types of causation which Socrates was so careful to distinguish came to be known as mechanical (or efficient) causation, that is causation by antecedent events and final causation which is causation by ends and purposes. So important is this distinction that John Baillie, from whom the account of the *Phaedo* above is taken, considers it to be the most important single passage in the whole of Western philosophy (Baillie 1951 pp 11–15). This notion of purposive activity (in process thought) applies not just to conscious activity but, as well, to mental activity that is not conscious. We are not attributing consciousness to atoms but are attributing something akin to mentality. We are saying that the fact that mentality exists in the universe in humans, the potentialities for it must have existed at the Big Bang and thereafter. It follows that the potentiality for mentality must exist in the whole universe that arose from the Big Bang. Of course potentialities are not always realised. It would be unwisely anthropomorphic to attribute conscious feelings to atoms, but this is not what process thought proposes. It does propose that something akin to mentality, such as final causation, is attributable to atoms; hence the term pansubjectivity (Cobb).

Maybe there are not many people in the world who think this way. This should not surprise us. Nobel laureate biochemist Albert Szent Gyorgyi, commenting on creative scientific thinking, said it was to see what everyone has seen but to think what no one has thought. Millions have seen apples fall from trees, but Newton's observation led him to the principle of gravitation. Millions had seen lamps swinging in churches, but Galileo's observation of them led him to formulate the principle of the pendulum and thence to the invention of clocks. Millions had seen plants and animals in nature but Charles Darwin's observations led him to formulate the theory of evolution by natural selection and thence the transformation of modern biology.

Critical observations combined with way-out imagination leads to discovery not only in science but in religion and philosophy as well. The philosopher AN Whitehead used his mathematical view of the world and his profound understanding of human experience, which included religion, to formulate a worldview that was radical and transformational. The process of radical discovery with new ideas 'nearly always' said Whitehead (1933b p 60) 'have a certain aspect of foolishness when they are first produced'. Biologist CH Waddington told me of a distinguished physicist who said he was not interested in new theories of quantum physics unless they looked crazy! In my list of biologists in Chapter 1 Sewall Wright, Haldane, Waddington and Agar are pansubjectivists. In my list of philosophers of religion, in addition to Whitehead, the pansubjectivists are Hartshorne, Cobb, Griffin, Williams and Barbour.

There is nothing in the way of proof that is incontestable in what I have to say. What then is the reason for accepting one view over another? Whitehead believed that the final tests of speculative concepts are their applicability and adequacy to experience and the coherence with one another. This is the principle of harmony.

The Whiteheadian proposition of pansubjectivism is that human experiences such as anticipation and purpose is but one end of a mode which stretches way down the scale of entities that are less complex. What is the evidence for that? Consider an Amoeba. It is an organism consisting of a single cell. Some species of Amoeba live in ponds where they feed on bacteria by engulfing them. They move around by sending out projections called pseudopodia, meaning false feet, into the world around them. Some of these projections can be retracted while others stretch out in all directions, some engulfing bacteria, others rejecting wastes. It appears they learn to make choices and exhibit strategies toward a desired end. They have their own degree of self-determination. We have cells in our body that are 'amoeboid' such as the white blood cells, the macrophages. They send out pseudopodia that engulf bacteria and other foreign bodies. Nerve cells are highly modified amoeboid cells. Some have enormously elongated pseudopodia-like projections, which serve as nerve fibres that conduct nerve impulses. They are called axons. As axons grow they send out thin, hair-like projections that explore the area around the tip of the growing axon. Some stretch out and make contact with muscles and glands whose activities they can trigger. Together they form a network of cells in the brain and spinal cord. The behaviour of Amoeba and amoeboid cells lead us to postulate that they have experiences or feelings. They may not be much like ours, but to say they are absolutely different is merely to say we have difficulty in imagining what it is like to be an Amoeba or an amoeboid cell in our bodies. We have less difficulty in imagining what it is like to be a dog. If Amoeba were the size of a dog we would have no more difficulty in imagining what it is to be an Amoeba than what it is like to be a dog. What is needed is imagination. It is more difficult to imagine what it is like to be an atom or an electron, but the principle of analogy remains the same. Why draw a line somewhere between a dog and an electron? The proposition of process thought is that no line is to be drawn. In order to cross this non-existing line imagination is needed. And that is in short supply.

There is more in the human than in the Amoeba. Hence the proposition that we shall form a truer concept of the evolutionary process when we study it from its end rather than from its beginning. This is the important principle of interpreting the lower in terms of the higher. This is top-down causation as opposed to bottom-up causation (interpreting the higher in terms of the lower). A universe which contains the personal should not be interpreted on a lower scale. When it comes to atoms and molecules the words 'attract', 'repel' (and the like) are still appropriate though used less. But why is this so? Whitehead thinks it is sheer illusion to suppose that there is some other way to imagine how these entities 'feel'. Newton had no hesitation in using the words 'attract' and 'repel' to describe chemical affinities. For Whitehead matter is understood as a form of mentality. This is not so way out. Buddhism accepts this, so does Hinduism and to some extent Plato and later philosophers such as Gottfried Leibnitz and CS Peirce (Hartshorne 1971). Proponents of this view do not claim that they can prove that all actual entities, from humans to quarks, have experience. They present this as a hypothesis that overcomes otherwise insoluble mysteries such as the relation between body and mind (see for example Griffin 1998).

Process thought makes the distinction between billiard-ball type entities and entities that exist by virtue of their inner relationship with each other, such as the love between two people. The terms 'experience' and 'process' can be used together. The radical idea of process thought is that the world is not made of substances but of events or processes which are called 'experiences'. Hence the title of Whitehead's most famous book *Process and Reality*. Notions of subjectivity and process apply all down the line from humans to quarks. Everything experiences in its own right or if it is an aggregate (eg, a rock) it consists of entities such as atoms that experience. All entities have a subjective aspect. Rocks and computers have merely an aggregational unity, not a subjective unity.

Besides the centrality of pansubjectivism from quarks to humans in process thought, it has a second major principle. Conventional wisdom is that only one kind of data enters our minds. It comes through the five senses. The nature described by science as we know it is in a different order of being from nature that includes the subjective.

Two kinds of perception

Whitehead agrees with Socrates that we perceive two kinds of data: sensuous and non-sensuous. The 'sensationalist' doctrine of perception is equated with sense-perception. Conventional wisdom is that sense perception is the fundamental way in which we are related to our world. It is the basis of all our knowledge of the world. Seeing, smelling, hearing, touching and tasting are the five routes of all our knowledge of the objective world. There are, in this view, no other routes to knowing the world. However, we ourselves have perceptions that are non-sensory such as of values and some claim of God in religious experience. We also feel the feelings of previous experiences in memory, which is non-sensory. Anticipation or purpose are non-sensory relations. Most of us go about our world with subconscious presuppositions that influence our beliefs and behaviour. And there may be other sorts of non-sensory perception such as telepathy. Further, if all actual entities experience, not just those with sense organs, there must be non-sensory modes of perception. Science traditionally deals only with knowledge that comes through the five senses. Hence such science deals with only half the evidence provided by human experience.

It is incredible to common sense that the only things that have any importance – namely feelings and qualities – are the things to be omitted from reality. The important is not real! This was the central clash I found between religion and science as a teenager studying science for the first time. My resolution of the conflict came when a friend Kenneth Newman, who was a lecturer in ethics at the University of Adelaide and a member of the Student Christian Movement, urged me to read AN Whitehead's *Science and the Modern World*. This gave me a non-materialist way of viewing the world together with an alternative to Christian fundamentalism which I was also discovering from another source: the thought of Harry Emerson Fosdick. Fosdick was my stepping stone to the thought of later liberal theologians such as Paul Tillich. Fosdick had fought his way through the fundamentalism of his youth to rational faith. He was charged with heresy. He responded that he would be ashamed to live in this generation and not be a heretic. This was the time, said Reinhold Niebuhr, when the old evangelical piety of American Protestantism, so vital in its earlier form and so potent in taming an advancing frontier, had hardened into a graceless biblicism and legalism. In addition to introducing me to Whitehead and fostering Fosdick, my mentor Kenneth Newman introduced me to Nicholai Hartmann's *Ethics* especially volume two on moral values. This was my introduction to ethical values that became so important in my thinking about values and their influence as understood in process thought. I found empathy in Hartmann's 'richness of experience' that tends now to be replaced by the phrase 'quality of life' which in turn is being superseded by 'the flourishing of life'. Hartmann made ethics live, as for example, when he said that to live apathetically from moment to moment amid abundance, is nothing short of sin.

Alfred North Whitehead
(Photograph by Richard Carver Wood, courtesy
Harvard University Archives)

The procedures of science, that concentrate on information from the five senses, are entirely justifiable provided we recognise the limitations involved. In one sense the abstraction has been a happy one in that it has allowed the simplest things to be considered first (Whitehead 1938 p 154). But when science, as we know it, deals with very complex issues, such as consciousness, its traditional methodology though appropriate for unravelling the outer aspects is, as yet, inadequate for understanding the subjective or inner aspect of consciousness. There is an enlightened alternative to exclusive mechanism that is excitingly being developed by process thought. It renders substantial justice to both schemes of thought. Hartshorne refers to it as a 'higher synthesis'.

To summarise the process position:

1. The entities of the world are not bits of stuff like tiny billiard balls. They are events, processes or experiences. Whitehead calls them 'occasions of experience' to be contrasted with the classical notion (of atoms) that he calls 'vacuous actualities'. These occasions of experience are the really real things that compose the evolving universe.

2. Perception of the world involves not only the five senses (sensationalism), but also non-sensory perception. Modern science has developed strong ties to both mechanism and sensationalism. The concept of an objective world and a subjective world consequent upon the two sorts of perception becomes critical in considering God's role discussed in chapter 6.

Centrality of experience

The doctrine of a feeling world is vastly different from the doctrines of modernism and deconstructive postmodernism. Instead of all entities being static and unchanging they are continually changing, becoming themselves by establishing internal relations with entities in their environment. A statue preserves its shape whereas a fountain performs it. One is static. The other is in process.

What do we mean by experience when this word is used for quarks and humans? It was caricatured when geneticist Theodosius Dobzhansky accused me of believing that atoms had brains! Others have said pansubjectivity attributes thoughts to rocks (concerning rocks see later). The doctrine does not mean that all actual entities (eg, atoms and cells) have consciousness. It means that they have something analogous to feeling, which is subjective. We should start by acknowledging the one thing of which we are most certain, our own experience. That could lead us to say with

René Descartes: 'I *feel* therefore I am.' We then go further than Descartes and ask when did feelings first appear in the evolution of the universe? Only two possible answers have been proposed. One is to say that nothing had feelings until birds or mammals or some other group of living organisms appeared late on the evolutionary scene. That is to believe in miracles. The other answer is to say there was no first appearance of feelings. Subjectivity was there all along. This theory turns the mechanistic argument on its head. The pansubjectivist model is the living organism rather than the lifeless machine. Instead of the higher (human beings) being interpreted solely in terms of the lower (classical atoms) comes the principle of interpreting the lower in terms of the higher. As physicist John A Wheeler asked rhetorically: 'Here is a man so what must the universe be?' The answer is that the universe is not composed of 'mere matter' but of mind-stuff. Our five senses lead us astray if they are considered to be the only source of our information. They are the main source of information for science, but a meaning for life needs to incorporate information from all sources. Here is the principle of interpreting the lower in terms of the higher. There is more in the human being than in the Amoeba. We shall form a truer concept of the creation if we study it from its end rather than solely from its beginning.

Objections to pansubjectivism

Griffin (1998 pp 92–8) discusses eight common objections to pansubjectivism. I believe he effectively refutes each one and presents nine valid reasons that support pansubjectivism (pp 89–92). A major error that opponents to pansubjectivism make is a 'category mistake' by claiming that mind *emerges* from no mind (Griffin 1998 pp 64–7). Such is to claim the emergence of an inside (mind) from things that have only outsides. The qualities of liquidity, solidity, saltiness and wetness, as experienced through our sense organs, can appropriately be described as examples of emergence as this term is used in evolution, hence properties for others. A biological example is the emergence of legs from fins. Both are of the same category namely things as seen from the outside. We do not suppose that water molecules feel wet to themselves. Wetness is a quality that appears to us. Experience cannot be listed in that category. To do so, Griffin argues, is to make a category mistake. In the evolutionary process mentality must be immanent or implicit in that from which it emerges. It must be in some manner present from the first. It was this proposition that convinced geneticists Sewall Wright and Waddington of pansubjectivity. Parallel to the evolution of the external world is an evolution of mentality.

Some objectors argue that pansubjectivity is anthropomorphic, that is attributing characteristics of human beings to things that cannot possibly possess them. The objectors confuse the distinction between mentality and consciousness, which I have already stressed. Consciousness is a feature of the lives of many animals including ourselves. But it is presumably absent from the lower end of the animal kingdom and plants. However, mentality is possible without consciousness. We recognise in ourselves unconscious dimensions in much that goes on in our nervous systems. We have experiences that are not conscious. Further it needs to be recognised that for all practical purposes, mentality, freedom, choice and decision are minimal in the inorganic realm. But there is all the world of a difference between the concepts of an atom without mentality and one with just a whiff of mentality and self-determination. To fail to recognise this is to commit what Hartshorne (1997 p 166) calls the 'zero fallacy'. The zero degree, or total absence, is knowable only if there is a known finite minimum of the property. Thus light intensity may be reduced to one photon. Less than that is no light. But how can we be dogmatic that there is zero self-determination in an atom? If you incline to say that this is all very academic I reply that a world of atoms with zero mentality is vastly different from one with minimal mentality. CS Peirce (one of the founders of modern process thought) called mentality the 'fountain of existence'. Zero is different from the tiniest bit of something. Hartshorne (1997 p 12) asks: 'What is the evidence that could tell us that atoms have zero mentality?' His reply is: 'there is none'.

Ecological worldview of pansubjectivism

In the process view all individual entities from quarks to human beings are internally related to their environments. Instead of invoking the machine as the world-model, we invoke the living organism. It is made up of living entities called cells, which have a life-history. For example each embryonic cell begins its life like every other embryonic cell with the same DNA. Eventually some become muscle cells, others become nerve cells and so on. What they become depends upon their surrounding cells. By contrast, in a factory or a cathedral the bricks or building blocks are the same whether they are in the walls or the ceiling. An entity, be it an atom or a human being, is what it is by virtue of its relations to other entities. All individual entities from quarks to humans are 'members one of another'. It is an ecological declaration of *interdependence*. The doctrine of independent building blocks is still widespread, despite the fact that modern physics has rejected it. The world of quantum physics is nothing like machinery. In a sense we are living at the end of an epoch whose chief architects were Isaac Newton, René Descartes, Galileo Galilei and John Locke.

First-person and third-person views

William James was strongly convinced of pansubjectivity. He prophesied that future generations may well look back at modern science in amazement for its systematic exclusion of 'the only form of thing that we directly encounter': human experience (Griffin et al 1993 p 108). In ourselves we have a piece of nature that we know from the inside as well as from the outside. Reductionist views miss what consciousness feels like from the inside. This is our first-person view of the world. Other people can only have a third-person view of us. Most of us assume that other animals such as dogs and cats have a first 'person' experience of some sort. We need an interpretation of 'experience' says Hartshorne 'that will apply all down the line' from humans to quarks. 'The insentient and mechanical [toward the bottom of the line] is a mere appearance or special case of the sentient' (Hartshorne 1953 pp 132–3). King Lear asks Gloucester how he sees the world. Gloucester, who is blind, answers, 'I see it feelingly.'

The centrality of experience of feelings in pansubjectivism could hardly be given more emphasis than Whitehead's declaration 'apart from the experience of subjects there is nothing, nothing, nothing, bare nothingness' (1929 p 167). Ours is a feeling world.

Are there then two ways of knowing, one concerned with the outer or third-person view and the other concerned with the inner first-person view? History seems to have given the view from outside to science and the view of the within to philosophy and religion. This gives us at best a two-sided stereoscopic vision of nature, but at worst a dualistic view of nature or what Whitehead called the bifurcation of nature. We need a view that will transcend this dichotomy. The apartheid solution is no solution. I would hope that the first-person experience and the third-person description both become part of an extended form of scientific understanding. This, I believe, was Whitehead's goal and his achievement, yet to a large extent not appreciated. So much did Whitehead achieve of this goal that Charles Hartshorne regarded pansubjectivism, as formulated by Whitehead, to be one of the great philosophical discoveries of our time enabling us to take the next step toward a unified concept of nature. But who is doing that now? It is an open question as to who is qualified to make judgments on these philosophical issues. Scientists tend to be uninformed of philosophy, while philosophers tend to be uninformed of science. What is needed is a mind that can encompass both in a profound way. Whitehead had the mind of a polymath. But it has been said that ours is a bad time for polymaths. By far the most notable carriers of the torch of process philosophy today are those involved in centres around the world and particularly at the Center for Process Studies in Claremont California, where scientists, philosophers and theologians work together to achieve a common vision.

Internal relations

Modern philosophy has left the nature of matter wholly mysterious, saying that we cannot know what it is in itself only how it appears to us, yet we ourselves know from within as well as from without (Griffin et al 1993 p 203). That is to say that we can indeed conjecture as to the nature of matter in itself. Central to this endeavour is the concept of internal relations. We can recognise two sorts of relations in human beings. I may be pushed around as an object by another object. That is an external relation. Or I may, for example, experience love or compassion with another person. That is an internal relation. I may say that I feel loved by God. That is an internal relation. I am a changed person when I experience internal relations. So too is my cat. St Thomas Aquinas recognised the distinction between internal and external relations in the 13th century. The principle concerns an animal, which we shall identify as a cat, standing by a pillar. The cat has a sense of wellbeing because the pillar protects it from the hot sun and wind and is a refuge from marauding dogs. The cat is internally related to the pillar but not the pillar to the cat. The cat's quality of life is definitely influenced by its relation to the pillar whereas nothing similar is obvious concerning the pillar. External relations are relations between substances. Internal relations involve subjects. External relations characterise substances. Internal relations have to do with events. External relations are incidental to the entity. A stone is a stone is a stone no matter what we do with it. The idea of an internal relation is of one that constitutes the character, even the existence of something. Tom Smith today is a different person from Tom Smith 10 years ago or even 10 hours ago. It is not only that he is older now. He is a different person by virtue of friendships he has made and thoughts which have dominated his life in those 10 days or years. Pansubjectivism sees this as a model all down the line from humans to atoms and quarks. An atom is what it is, not only by its constituents of electrons, protons and the like. It is what it is by virtue of its relations to its surrounding world. Common salt consists of sodium and chlorine atoms. According to classical materialism the sodium and chlorine atoms are unaffected by their combination. In principle all the properties of salt should be discoverable in sodium and chlorine investigated in isolation. But this in fact proves impossible. The events that make up sodium and chlorine atoms are affected by the entities in their environment. When these environments include each other in appropriate ratios the atoms exhibit properties they do not exhibit in other environments. Their internal relations are different. The events that make up the sodium and chlorine atoms are affected by their environment. Likewise, when certain arrangements of carbon, nitrogen and hydrogen atoms together with a few others, exhibit properties that we recognise by the name 'enzyme', we have discovered something new about the nature of these atoms. They have potentialities we did not know existed until we discovered what enzymes consist of. Atoms are affected by their relationships. Since these relationships participate in the constitution of atoms they are internal relations. In this concept the entities are altered by the relationships into which they enter. The entities A, B and C are different in isolated states from their condition when interrelated. Whitehead (1929 p 50) said that the philosophy of internal relations was mainly devoted to the task of making clear the notion of 'being present' in another entity, for which he used the term 'prehension'. The constitution of entities by their relationships or happenings is expressed in Whitehead's much quoted statement 'The many become one, and are increased by one' (1929 p 21). The many are not one. They become one. There are, for example, many events in the nerve cells (or neurones) in the brain that lead to a moment of consciousness. The many neuronal events become the one event of consciousness. This adds one to the number of events. It is a case of one together with one makes three. The experience of consciousness is not made up of neuronal events added together, one to the other. They are integrated into a single coherent experience with its own memory and its own anticipations. There are many different sorts of actual entities such, for example, as atoms. It is the destiny of many atomic events to enter into a novel unitary event such as a complex molecule. The novel molecule is an addition to the world. It exists by virtue of the internal relations of the original atoms. It is an example of emergence of something new. It is the destiny of the new molecule to be united with other molecules to form new entities and so on without end! Likewise in quantum physics the quantum whole is not simply a sum of its parts. The principle which has been called the combination problem of explaining how, for example, a moment of consciousness arises out of a myriad of neuronal events, is one of the difficult problems in pansubjectivism. It is also an instance of what is ultimate reality. Whitehead's statement 'The many become one, and are increased by one' (1929 p 21) is a universal principle of creativity and of cosmic evolution. The new unity is no mere rearrangement of old units. It is a new singular actuality. The evolving universe is a vast ecological system for the creation of novelty.

Instead of taking for granted that the world is composed of unchanging substances akin to Democritus' atoms we think instead of a world whose entities have the potentiality of becoming something different as their environment changes. Entities are necessarily altered by the relations they enter. On the other hand to mechanists relations do not alter the entities that are related. In general terms entities A, B and C are different in their isolated states from their condition when interrelated.

Purposive nature of experience

Experience has two components: feelings from the past (as in memories) and secondly feelings towards possible futures (as in anticipations). Whitehead has put this into a memorable phrase 'the present is the fringe of memory tinged with anticipation'. The past is part of the present just as is the future. Life is enjoyment of emotion derived from the past and aimed at the future. Every day each of us hopefully has anticipation of things to be achieved. We cannot understand our lives without the idea of aim or purpose guiding us (Birch 1990). We get bored and long for something that will restore zest to life. We then experience satisfaction. Anticipation and purpose do this.

> The conduct of human affairs is entirely dominated by our recognition of foresight determining purpose, and purpose issuing in conduct. Almost every sentence we utter and every judgment we form, presupposes our unfailing experience of this element of life. The evidence is so overwhelming, the belief so unquestioning, the evidence of language so decisive, that it is difficult to know where to begin in demonstrating it [Whitehead 1966 p 13].

Whitehead proceeds to give examples of the role of purpose in our lives and the attempts of some investigators to design experiments to substantiate the belief that animal activities (including our own) are not motivated by any purpose. He concludes (p 16) that 'scientists animated by the purpose of proving that they are purposeless constitute an interesting subject for study'.

Anticipation includes the idea of the urge to live. The urge to live is toward novelty with ever richer, more intensive and more satisfying experiences. Seeking intensity is not mere preservation, although it includes preservation. Its antithesis is depression and suicide. The World Health Organization estimates that depression is the world's leading cause of disability. So at any one time there are a lot of people in the world whose intensity of living is pretty low. For some, the consequence is suicide. In the UK significantly more people killed themselves on Monday than on any other day of the week. This was blamed on Monday being a new beginning. In the

US most suicides are in the month of May; one of the most pleasant months of the year. Not to feel what your colleagues around you are feeling can have devastating psychological effects.

'The art of life,' says Whitehead 'is *first* to be alive, *secondly* to be alive in a satisfactory way, and *thirdly* to acquire an increase in satisfaction' (1966 p 8). This has a certain obviousness even to the point of banality. But it has a profound meaning. The urge to live is to be alive. Lose that urge and you die. So I think it can be truly said that evolution of life leads to life abundant. The urge to live has three components: creative activity, self-enjoyment and aim. Every moment something new is achieved. It depends upon the focus provided by aim. It is self-enjoyable which itself extends the aim.

Can we discern purpose and anticipation (the urge to live) in non-human animals? To find them there is to open the way for a wider picture in which anticipation, purpose, valuation and satisfaction (self-enjoyment) can find a status along with mechanical causal relationships. The world then becomes full of subjects that are experiencing entities (Birch 1995). An indication of purposiveness in the behaviour of living organisms is the familiar fact that the sequence of acts by which the goal is attained is not always the same. The completed spider's web, the wasp's nest, the act of mating are attained by a train of acts different in detail on different occasions. Thorpe (1958 p 231) gives numerous examples of such activities by wasps. The hunting wasp *Ammophila* hunts for caterpillars to bring to its newly-made nest where it will then lay an egg. Sometimes the caterpillars are too heavy to be brought back on the wing and are then dragged for hundreds of metres across rough terrain and over every conceivable obstacle. From time to time the wasp may leave the prey and take short flights as though surveying the area. Prior to the hunt the nest has been made. It is made in the soil and consists of a vertical shaft a couple of centimetres long. When the shaft is completed it is temporarily closed by loosely filling in the entrance with soil and small stones. When the wasp returns to the nest with the paralysed caterpillar. She deposits it near the entrance, opens the nest, carries the caterpillar down and lays an egg on it. She then closes the nest with much more care now that there is a caterpillar inside. It is then virtually impossible for the human eye to distinguish the entrance from the surroundings. Soon after she begins to dig a new nest, which may take a day or more. After the nests are completed and stored with caterpillars the wasp makes return visits, opens the nest and makes an inspection. Depending on what she finds she may go and fetch fresh caterpillars, which she places in the nest with an egg. If the experimenter opens the nest and places a strange object in it such as a caterpillar with an egg already in it the wasp pulls it out of the cell and throws it away. If the object was an *Ammophila* larva she would often capture another caterpillar for the larva to feed on. The wasp may make as many as three nests, which she constructs and attends at the same time. Experiments have been conducted with *Eumenid* wasps in which the wasp has been induced to break off the routine of making the mud nests in order to repair artificial damage to the cells. If a rent is made in the side of a cell it may be some time before the wasp recognises the damage. When she does she flies away and collects a pellet of mud and repairs the damage to the cell. She may repair the hole by a method different from that of closing the mouth of the cell. These are purposive activities in the sense that each step in the sequence that leads to a completed nest appears to be self-rewarding or self-satisfying. One goal having been completed leads to the next one. The purpose of the insect is evident at each step in the sequence. The fact that the whole sequence leads to survival of the species is not the purpose of the wasp. That is a consequence of natural selection. No doubt some of the activities of the wasp may be interpreted mechanistically. But not all. It is important to recognise that the chemical and physical events studied by the biologist are the biological correlates of activities which have the mental component of purpose. The same applies to human behaviour.

Embryonic development from egg to newborn can be seen in the same light. Agar (1951) interprets each step in embryonic development as behaviour. The fertilised egg 'insists' on changing. The only way to stop it changing is to kill it. As it changes it becomes more complex. Embryonic development consists of a long train of actions by many agents each of which may be interpreted as purposive. But there is no need to suppose that the creature at the beginning of the complex sequence of events envisages the final goal of that activity any more than does the nest-making wasp. Its purpose is immediate like the separate stages of completing the wasp's nest. I was introduced to the role of purpose in animal behaviour and embryonic development by zoologist WE Agar who, well before any other biologist, was interpreting animal life within a framework of process thought.

There is good reason to suppose that goal-like activities are accompanied by feelings of satisfaction or the urge to live. We might find this difficult to imagine in the case of a wasp. But anyone who has lived with a kitten is struck by the kitten's vigorous activity to do with discovering new places, finding new toys to play with, finding a cosy place for sleeping and enjoying food. The normal kitten seems to enjoy life, even ecstatically at times! With this perspective we can look at the whole history of life and discern there an increase in the richness of the experience of life with the increasing complexity of life from single cells to ourselves. Survival of the fittest is a principle of evolution. But fitness is not simply survival. It includes the urge to live without which there would be little survival in life.

Traditionally science and also theology have accepted a total separation between the objective and subjective worlds. So a subjective reality such as purpose and anticipation could have nothing to do with what can be observed objectively. The divorce between objectivity and subjectivity is an impasse for our common-sense perception of the world, shows that our subjective intentions, for example, result in action in the objective world. Process thought has developed the most comprehensive attempt ever made to bring the two together. Its picture is a radical departure from mechanistic causality as the one principle which at present dominates science, particularly biological science. Values, intentions and anticipation are not only features of human life but are, in process thought, considered to be aspects of all entities in the sequence of humans to quarks. One would think that biology would lead the way in this venture of thought but that is not the case. Quantum physics does. Maybe physicists working in biology will change the scene. The great physicist, Richard Feynman, has said 'the science of biology is the most active, most exciting and most rapidly developing science today in the West' (Feynman 1998 p 53). He was referring to the advances of molecular biology. Is it possible these advances, like non-mechanistic progress in modern physics, could lead to a reinterpretation of life that is non-mechanistic?

Process thought presses for such a change in direction of thinking in biology. The urge to live is characteristic of all animals we are familiar with. They, with human beings, strive to reunite with that from which they feel separated; they desire food, movement, growth, involvement with others and sexual union. The fulfilment of these desires is accompanied by pleasure. Tillich has much emphasised fulfilment of life as extreme happiness and at the same time the end of happiness. Without the tension of separation there is no love and no life. This is the urge to live that forever raises new tensions between that which is and that which ought to be. The urge to live is the striving to reunite the individual with that to which the individual belongs and from which the individual is separated. Life is separation and reunion. There is hardly a more striking example of this than what happened in Tolstoy's life after he had completed his own greatest novels: *War and Peace* and *Anna Karenina*. He suffered an emotional and spiritual collapse. Having completed the novels, a large part of himself which was incorporated in the lives of practically everyone he wrote about, then ceased to exist. Having used himself up in one capacity (in the novel) he could not rediscover himself in his moment to moment experience (Wilson 1988 p 302).

Values

A philosophy of life leads to an ethic of living which is characterised by the particular values it promotes. There are a great variety of ethical stances (see Fox 2006). It is commonly held that no one can claim what is right and wrong. Ethics is just a matter of opinion. Good versus bad gives way to an 'I'm OK, you're OK' attitude. There are no standards for the good life. Are there then, no particular values that make the good person and the good citizen? Is all relative?

In process thought there is an objectivity of values. What represents the ideal of a healthy pine tree would be known to botanists, whoever and wherever they might be. They would agree that there are unhealthy or mutilated pine trees that are poor representatives of the species. Everything has a nature and its virtue is to fulfil that nature. In humans there are those who do not represent what it is to be a fulfilled human. Self-fulfilment is the relevant concept. We experience self-fulfilment to varying degrees. There is a real better and a real worse. There are psychopathic humans (such as Nero, Attila the Hun and Adolf Hitler) who don't simply lack certain values but who seem to be evil in intent. They are defective or flawed human beings.

Moral education, said Whitehead in his 'Aims of education and other essays', is impossible apart from the habitual vision of greatness. My exemplars of such a habitual vision include Jesus, Socrates, St Francis, St Theresa and Albert Schweitzer. For Socrates and Plato the virtuous person tells truth fearlessly, takes responsibility for their actions, courage is always praised, also humility, thrift, conscientiousness, justice and the ability to control one's passions. These are some of the values uppermost in the society that Socrates and Plato espoused (MacIntyre 1981). Equality for women, according to Bertrand Russell (1956 p 122), few ever thought of claiming until the French Revolution, except Plato. For Christians, Jesus and those who reflect his life represent fulfilled humanity. The central value for Jesus was love of neighbour, self and God. He emphasised the importance of the individual so far as values are concerned. When one sheep of the flock of 100 is lost it is the one that is lost that is valued over all others and commands attention over all until it is found.

Process thought leads to this summary of ethical behaviour (Henning 2005 p 146):

i. to maximise the intensity and harmony of one's own experience;

ii. to maximise the intensity and harmony of experience of everything within one's sphere of influence.

Happiness comes in the fulfillment of one's own essential nature. If I were asked what has given me most happiness I would say that high on my list would be trying do what I think I couldn't do and then doing it. It is a making real one's potential as yet unrealised. This can become reality when someone believes in you and your hidden possibilities when you did not believe in them yourself. The message is to become what you really are.

In the last chapter I introduced Whitehead's proposal that the art of life is 'first to be alive, secondly to be alive in a satisfactory way, and thirdly to acquire an increase in satisfaction' (1966 p 8). Values flow from these affirmations. Whitehead went on to say that reason is the factor in experience that directs and criticises the urge toward the attainment of these values. And as David Hume said: 'reason is, and ought to be, the slave of passions'. The locus of value is feelings; that is experience (Ferre 2001 p 113). We need to follow our conscience in the moment of choice of values. But we do not need to settle for the conscience of a child or adolescent. Early experience is childish. As one matures so does one's experience, bringing with it a sense of assurance.

Value is, as Whitehead suggested, intensity of richness of experience. It is reasonable to suppose that an Amoeba's experience is less rich than that of a human being. It is reasonable to go beyond this proposition and identify an order of increasing value in evolution. In so doing we are not postulating a straight-line evolution of richness of experience, but a general increase from Amoeba to fish to reptiles and mammals and within mammals from kangaroos to humans. This is a speculation, but one consistent with a Whiteheadian view of evolution in which alongside the evolution of the body is an evolution of mentality. The objective evolves with the subjective. The subjective is causal in so far as elements such as purpose are causal, as I have suggested.

We experience a tension between what we are and what we feel we ought to be. The tension is twofold. It is a longing for the higher good which is represented by the Greek word *eros*. Secondly, it includes a lure from beyond ourselves and is called *agape*. We don't invent values. We appropriate them. Love is not to be an off and on affair but a continuous relationship. This is spoken of in the New Testament as 'praying without ceasing'. Taken literally this is nonsense. It points to considering every moment as filled with the divine values. *Eros* is a desiring and egocentric love aimed at some satisfaction. Pleasure and self-actualisation are contravened when deliberately sought as ends in themselves. Psychiatrist Viktor Frankl was presented with a boomerang when he visited Australia. He had assumed that a boomerang returns to the thrower. He discovered that it returns to the thrower only when the thrower has missed the target. Similarly, he said, we turn to ourselves narcissistically and are concerned with self only after we have missed our mission and failed to find meaning in life which comes by committing self to a cause greater than the self. Selfishness is not living as one wishes to live. It is expecting others to live as one wishes them to live. Its opposite is to wish for others what is fulfilling for them. We should not be sorry for ourselves like the youth in unrequited love standing on a high storey ledge. As he teeters he threatens his girlfriend below that he will jump unless she does what he wants. Let's not be sorry for ourselves. Let our sorrow be for others.

Agape is theocentric and selfless. It is God's love coming to humans. The purpose of God is the attainment of value in the world. God confronts what is actual in the world with what is possible for it (Whitehead 1927 pp 87, 144). I learned from professor Henry N Wieman (1946) of the Divinity School in the University of Chicago the distinction between created goods (values) and the creative source of good. The human problem, as Wieman sees it, is to shape human conduct so that creative good can be released to produce maximum good. But much of human life hampers the full realisation of creative good as, for example, fear, distrust, deceit and hubris. Created goods can be destroyed. Creative good cannot be destroyed, but it can be obstructed. The created goods we call values are discovered by us rather than invented by us. They wait for us to become concrete in our lives. We are, says Wieman, made for creative transformation as a bird is made for flight. To be sure we are in a cage much of the time. The bars of the cage are the resistance to creative transformation.

Our image of human nature influences our assessment of human values. A mechanistic image leads to repression and puritanism. Worse it can lead to sadism as happened to Nazi SS guards in concentration camps who knew people as numbers. We make a mistake when we label people as having natures that are good or bad. Each one of us can be both. There is Scrooge before and Scrooge after, Saul before and Paul after. Baldur von Schirach, head of Hitler youth, was sentenced to 20 years in prison for crimes against humanity committed in Nazi Vienna. In death he discovered the ambiguity of life. On his gravestone are these words he requested to be there 'I was one of you'. For ten years I was involved in activities at the Wayside Chapel in Kings Cross, Sydney. This was a very special organisation of the Uniting Church concerned with dropouts, prostitutes, drug addicts and others on the edge of society. What impressed me most was that a dropout would find very quickly another dropout who could say to him I am one of you. The work of transformation began with this sort of sharing and identification. The crisis centre, open 24 hours, was manned primarily, not with experts, but with people who could say: 'I am one of you'. It worked. I received a letter recently from a dropout from New Zealand whom I met at the Wayside Chapel. He wanted to tell me he is now a professor of neurobiology in London. All we did was to set him on the path of self-discovery.

Whitehead (1966 p 10) saw that human reason includes that which Ulysses shares with the foxes and that which Plato shares with the gods. He argues for the reconciliation of both drives, presumably in the one person. According to Livingstone (1946 p 136) the Greeks were continuously fighting to keep their emotional temperament in subjection to reason. Plato in the *Phaedrus* figures the human soul as a charioteer, struggling with an unruly horse, his animal nature, striving to recall his memory of his vision of truth, of temperance, justice and beauty. Sometimes the struggle ended in defeat but others succeeded in reining in the rebellious horse to reach an Olympian peace. Sophocles, and probably Plato, were men of violent passions and only reached freedom after a long struggle with 'many mad tyrants'. Paul Tillich said he had to struggle with his *daemons* every morning before ten o'clock. The higher religions believe in the possibility of transformation from the bad to the good. It is called salvation, which literally means healing. Its opposite is called sin, which means missing the mark. We experience both.

In process thought creative good can be identified with God, especially the primordial nature of God (see later), though Wieman does not make this identification. Living organisms besides humans experience value because they have feelings, though they are not concerned with truth until linguistic capacities can be used in humans.

The commitment to value, such as courage and forgiveness, brings its own self-authenticating quality. Here stand I. I can do no other so help me God! Once grasped, these ideas appear self-evident. For the Christian the person of Jesus is universal for all humanity. This means that the values concretely real in his life speak to all human life whether he is recognised or not as the bearer of such values. Human cultures differ from place to place and across time. Yet William Shakespeare who lived in Elizabethan England speaks to modern man. Goethe's world was Weimar, but he too is universal. Despite cultural differences we recognise a common human nature with universal needs. Out of the culture of Athens came the Platonic philosophy of human nature and with it Plato's invention of the university which exists to this day all over the world.

But what is the authority that tells me whether or not I am right or wrong in my decisions? There is none. This is the Protestant Principle which I learned from Tillich:

> Every genuine Protestant is called upon to bear personal responsibility ... each Protestant, each layman, each minister has to decide for himself whether a doctrine is true or not, whether a prophet is a true or false prophet, whether power is demonic or divine. Even the bible cannot liberate him from this responsibility, for the bible is a subject of interpretation; there is no doctrine, no prophet, no priest, no power, which has not claimed biblical sanction for itself. For the Protestant, individual decision is inescapable [Tillich 1948 p 226].

Luther believed the Bible was his authority, thinking that all would interpret it in the same way. But people differed in their interpretation. So he appointed theologian Melanchthon as his interpreter. But other scholarly interpreters differed from Melanchthon. Who then is the authority?

Obedience to a hierarchical priesthood or the Bible is supplanted by the 'priesthood of all believers'. The individual conscience is guided by scripture and the religious community. The Protestant Principle is a most radical challenge to any person or organisation claiming ultimate authority. It is a challenge to those who flee to forms of authoritarianism such as fundamentalism. The Protestant Principle is an affirmation of daring courage. Luther, and consequently the whole of the Protestant world, broke away from the Roman church and 1500 years of Christian tradition. The authority of one God was replaced by the ultimate authority of the individual.

To act rightly is to love. St Augustine stressed an ethic of love: 'Love God,' he said 'and do as you please.' According to Whitehead (1929 p 343):

> Love does not emphasise the ruling Caesar, or the ruthless moralist, or the unmoved mover. It dwells upon the tender elements of the world, which slowly and quietly operate by love, and it finds purpose in the present immediacy of a kingdom not of this world. Love neither rules, nor is it unmoved; also it is a little oblivious as to morals. It does not look to the future; for it finds its own reward in the immediate present.

The 13th chapter of the first letter of Paul to the Corinthians tells first what love is not and then what love is. This latter part in JB Phillips' translation is as follows:

The love of which I speak is slow to lose patience. It looks for a way of being constructive. It is not possessive. It is neither anxious to impress nor does it cherish inflated ideas of its own importance. Love has good manners and does not pursue selfish advantage. It is not touchy. It does not compile statistics of evil or gloat over the wickedness of other people. On the contrary it is glad with all good men when truth prevails. Love knows no limits to its endurance, no end to its trust, no fading of its hope: it can outlast anything. It is, in fact, the one thing that still stands when all else has fallen ... In this life we have three great lasting qualities – faith, hope and love. But the greatest of them is love.

This is no easy way. One may have to struggle 40 days and 40 nights. When Buddhist professor DT Suzuki was asked in his 90s what was the secret of his longevity he replied 'I try not to get angry and I think I am improving.' We also need take heed of Reinhold Niebuhr's constant warning of our easy slide into hubris. As the Magnificat (Luke 1:46–55) says 'he has scattered the proud in the imagination of their hearts'. Perhaps the most difficult part of these times is to see what is needed in the global, political and economic context in which our lives are bound. In discussing these values in *The Republic* Plato argued that we are discussing no trivial matter, but how we ought to live (Singer 1993 p 8).

Value of nature
We have just discussed human values and indicated that all creatures have an intrinsic value, which may or may not be respected. The conservationist says we have a responsibility to look after nature because nature looks after us. That is to give nature an instrumental value, which is good so far as it goes. But

it doesn't go far enough. Pansubjectivism recognises a second value in nature. It is the intrinsic value of individual organisms (quite independent of their instrumental value). What then gives entities intrinsic value? I learned from John Cobb that it is feeling that gives entities their intrinsic value. From what I have already said this implies that there is a gradation of intrinsic value all down the line from humans to quarks. And within any category, such as humans, there is a gradation depending on the quality of life of the individual. It can be low in a person with advanced dementia as compared with a healthy, active person in possession of all his faculties. Pansubjectivism makes a difference as to how we view our world, not only other people, but also the world of our companion animals and all of nature (Birch 1993). We have to balance instrumental value with intrinsic value. An elephant has a positive instrumental value to humans when used for transporting logs. But that usage needs to be balanced by consideration for its wellbeing. Elsewhere an elephant may have a negative instrumental value when it damages crops. The inhumane solution is to get rid of such an elephant. The humane solution, that takes account of its intrinsic value, is to extend the neighbouring national park or transport the elephant into another area where it can live out its life without fear. This is being done in Africa where farming is encroaching on natural reserves. These ideas are developed in some detail in *Regaining Compassion: For humanity and nature* (Birch 1993) and in *Living with Animals* (Birch and Vischer 1997). In these two books the following questions are discussed: Do animals have minds? Do they reason? Are they conscious? Are they self-conscious? Do they suffer? Do they have rights?

Evolving cosmos

Cosmic evolution has the appearance of a struggle for integration and order against influences that tend to disorder. Wieman (1929 pp 213–19) conceived the evolution of the cosmos as an order and stability achieved at successive levels. There was a time, perhaps 20 billion years ago, when the association of elementary particles into atoms had achieved no stability. That epoch passed and the universe consisted of hydrogen atoms only. Yet the potentiality was within those atoms to produce the diversity of entities that exist in the world today from atoms to humans. One can contemplate that the universe may have come to a stop with a world of hydrogen atoms. It didn't. It went on to produce greater diversity. The association of atoms and molecules into living organisms was another frontier but as yet not so firmly established as the world of atoms and molecules. Here misfits occurred as the first cells, perhaps in a tropical sea, some billions of years ago, struggled to survive. Some succeeded. The organisation of cells into complex organisms may have taken millions of years to achieve. Stability does exist, yet it is not as secure as the association of atoms and molecules. Indeed the ultimate fate of 99.99 per cent of all species is to become extinct. Yet life survived. It led to a new organisation of conscious individuals in human societies. Here we find integration woefully inadequate for the expression of the potentialities of such societies. Why should chaos and disintegration be so widespread and perilous in human societies? Human life is now the fighting frontier of the progressive integration of the universe so far as we know. Here the cosmic venture is under way. To have got this far there have been and are great risks. Here the possibility of richness of experience is greater than at any of the previous levels of creation. At the same time the cost in terms of suffering and unfulfilled lives is greater than at any other level. This is the principle that the possibilities for good cannot be increased without also increasing the possibilities for evil. If this were a lifeless universe there would be no pain, no sickness, no sin, no injustice, no oppression, no death. Life has introduced disorder into the world. Human organisations provide the conditions for progress and also for regression. The key to the gates of heaven is given to everyone. The same key opens the gates of hell. We are participants in the adventure of an unfinished universe.

The existence of an ordered and creative society is maintained by a perilously slight margin of sensitivity and control. The creative advance of any generation rests upon the responsiveness of a pitifully small margin of human responsiveness. 'The art of progress', says Whitehead (1929 p 339)

is to preserve order amid change and to preserve change amid order. Life refuses to be embalmed alive. The more prolonged the halt in some unrelieved system of order, the greater the crash of the dead society.

It is at this point that Reinhold Niebuhr's analysis of the ambiguities of human society, as we indicated earlier, becomes relevant. Even so, life on this planet will come to an end. What then are we to make of the value of cosmic evolution? It must be something that cannot be destroyed by death. To that we now turn.

6 MY PHILOSOPHY OF LIFE: PANENTHEISM

God

Questioning classical theism

The word 'God' is fraught with many meanings, some of which are erroneous and simplistic. Hartshorne (1962 pp 138–9) has argued that most errors about God are errors about the world (eg, the world conceived as a machine). Whitehead comments that the various doctrines about God have not suffered chiefly from their complexity, but from being simplistic. So confusing is the diversity of meanings of the word God that some theologians have called for a moratorium on the word. I indicated earlier that Paul Tillich substitutes the phrase 'ultimate concern' for God. Diverse too is the relevance of the word 'religion' in our time. The first word to be spoken about religion to the people of our time, says Tillich (1948 p 185) must be a work spoken against religion.

> Religion has often been nothing more than the superficial consecration of some situation or action which was neither judged nor transformed by this consecration. Religion has consecrated the feudal order and its own participation in it without transcending it. Religion has consecrated nationalism without transforming it. Religion has consecrated democracy

without judging it. Religion has consecrated war and the arms of war without using its spiritual arms against wars. Religion has consecrated peace and the security of peace without disturbing this security with its spiritual threat. Religion has consecrated the bourgeois ideal of family and property without judging it and has consecrated systems of exploitation of men by men without transcending them; on the contrary it has used both of them for its own benefit.

Classical theism, as found in orthodox and also fundamentalist Christianity, ascribes to God such characteristics as omnipotence, omniscience and the supernatural. God's relation to the world is magical and coercive and is conceived in terms of an obsolete pre-scientific worldview. This is the concept of God that Richard Dawkins (2006) wrote about in his book, *The God Delusion*. The Christian creeds formulated in the 4th and 5th centuries summarise these doctrines. God created the world. His son Jesus came down from heaven to redeem it and will come back again to judge it. Not a word about the life of Jesus between his birth and death. The makers of 4th century Christian creeds struggled to keep Jesus in our species.

God as 'ultimate concern' (Tillich) is that which transforms life. The only appropriate response to ultimate concern is 'with infinite passion'. Whenever we transcend the limits of our own being and move toward ultimate fulfilment there is ecstasy and passion.

One reason for the modern denial of any kind of cosmic mind is that all such notions become suspect by association with supernaturalism. This is why Nicholai Berdyaev, the Russian philosopher and theologian, says that he fights against God in the name of God. Pansubjectivism leads to a God who is neither omniscient, omnipotent, coercive, unchanging, unaffected by the world, nor supernatural. It is one of a variety of the dozen concepts of theism (Hartshorne and Reese 1953, Birch 1999). In classical theism God is the absolute ruler of the universe. Every event is predestined in accordance with God's will. All these attributes are questioned by process thought.

'There is,' says Whitehead (1929 p 343):

> in the Galilean origin of Christianity yet another suggestion ... It does not emphasise the ruling Caesar, or the ruthless moralist, or the unmoved mover. It dwells upon the tender elements in the world, which slowly and in quietness operate by love; and it finds purpose in the present immediacy of a kingdom not of this world. Love neither rules, nor is it unmoved; also it is a little oblivious as to morals. It does not look to the future; for it finds its own reward in the immediate present.

Classical theism is widely associated with the concept of the world as mechanism. The implication is that God is a mechanic. Process theism is part and parcel of a quite different world whose entities are responsive, that is experiential. Pansubjectivity and process theism go hand in hand. Hence the emphasis on the two together in what follows.

Process theism

In theistic process thought, God's activity is one of persuasion and compassion as exemplified in the life of Jesus. 'Behold I stand at the door and knock' is the image of God's relation to human beings. There is no forced entry, just patient persuading. We have our own degree of freedom to respond or not respond. The power of God is not coercive but persuasive. We have power over others through the value they find in our thought. The direct influence of God is analogous to the power of thought over thought, of feeling over feeling, but never to suppress all freedom. So too is this the image of God's relation to the rest of the creation. It implies that entities from quarks to atoms to cells and all the way up to humans have their own degree of freedom and self-determination, tiny though this might be for atoms. Yet they are not machines.

God's persuasion, as opposed to coercion, is not a voluntary self-limitation. This view is a half-way house to a God of omnipotence and has no place in genuine process thought. God in process thought could not choose from time to time to intervene coercively here and there in the world. There is an essential difference between a God who *has not* intervened except to produce an occasional virgin birth or physical resurrection and a God who *cannot* intervene. Martin Luther was clear about this. 'I call the omnipotence of God not that power by which he does not do many things he could do, but the actual power by which he potently does everything in everything.' In quoting this, Paul Tillich adds 'The absurd idea of a God who calculates whether he should do what he could do is removed by this idea of God as creative power' (Tillich 1967 p 248).

The fact that God's power is persuasive, not coercive, means that God is not unilaterally responsible for any event. God and the world are co-creators. Given the freedom of the creature to be persuaded or not to be persuaded, conflict is inevitable. That is a cost of creation. God's creativity works through the spontaneity and self-determination of the creatures. As Charles Kingsley said at the time of the dispute about evolution between Thomas Henry Huxley and Samuel Wilberforce, bishop of Oxford: 'God makes things that make themselves.' We now refer to this as the principle of self-organisation.

It is misleading to talk of 'divine design' or 'intelligent design'. Design has the connotation of a preconceived pattern or blueprint.

It is a highly dangerous doctrine as it eliminates freedom and so destroys the central concept of creativity. This argument applies to the so-called anthropic principle which in its strongest form argues that some 20 physical constants are finely tuned to the necessity of life. If their values were different life would not be possible. There are alternative explanations for so-called fine-tuning, notably the multi-universe hypothesis. This is the proposal that there are a multitude of universes at the same time as ours or at different times. The chances are that in one of them fine-tuning would happen by chance. An amusing and yet important critical account of the anthropic principle is given by Martin Gardner (1997 pp 41–9).

The ordering of the creation by God and the creatures can be likened to the role of the conductor and players in an orchestra. Each player interprets the score in his or her own way. But all are coordinated by the conductor who writes the score. Each musician interprets the score and is corrected or praised by the conductor who may have the whole performance in his head. God is the composer-conductor who is writing the score, perhaps only a few bars ahead of the orchestra's performance. Both composer-conductor and the players determine the final outcome.

Materialism doesn't work

Whitehead (1933b p 135) regarded it as inconceivable that the vacuous entities of the mechanistic or materialistic worldview could give rise to evolution at any level. An evolutionary philosophy is inconsistent with materialism:

> Evolution on the materialistic theory, is reduced to the role of being another word for the description of the changes of the external relations between portions of matter. There is nothing to evolve, because one set of external relations is as

good as any other set of external relations. There can merely be change, purposeless and unprogressive. But the whole point of the modern doctrine is the evolution of the complex organisms from antecedent states of less complex organisms. The doctrine thus cries aloud for a conception of organism as fundamental for nature.

Here Whitehead contrasts the materialist concept of the relationship of objects that have only external relations with evolution which involves internal relations between subjects. The materials of a materialistic philosophy are incapable of evolution.

How God acts in the world

I am indebted to John Cobb (personal communication) for the following conception of how God acts in the world, in its being and in its evolution. If we look for divine causality in the objective world to which science usually limits itself, that is the sphere of sense data, we cannot find it. There is no intelligible concept of God's acting as an agent in this objective sphere and any proposal that God intervenes in the objective world is anathema to science. God's role is in the sphere of the subjective. This is best known to us in the way religious people think of God in their lives inspiring and calling one forward. To locate God in the world of subjects is much more intelligible than to try and locate God in the world of objects such, for example, as the world revealed by classical physics or biological evolution. They present us with pictures revealed by the senses. God is a subject and acts not on objects but on subjects. Does this then dismiss the relevance of God to the 'real' world? Not at all. Objects do not exist simply in themselves. The actual world in process thought has its subjective side (as I have been at pains to stress). So we look for divine causality in that realm. Divine causality is creative in the subjective world and that creativity is reflected in the world of objects, as for example in creative evolution as new forms come into existence. So it would be true to say that God indirectly has an influence on objects. That is a story that has yet to be fully told.

Before Whitehead, William James said: 'If evolution is to work smoothly, consciousness in some shape must have been at the very origin of things' (Griffin et al 1993 p 100). The 'shape' is unconscious mentality of some sort.

Evolution is not simply the rearrangement of bits of matter, one bit being added to another, but an integration of feeling entities in new ways that make new entities. If we were able to see the evolutionary sequence from inside we would discern an evolution of mentality from beginnings in the inanimate world to its flourishing in mammals.

Evolution from a Whiteheadian perspective is an evolution of subjects. A subject helps to create is own environment. It may by its behaviour choose its environment and so change the direction of natural selection. At least in the higher mammals, purpose becomes influential in behaviour. Process thought argues for purpose as a factor from the beginning in the form of some degree of self-determination and creativity in the so-called inanimate world. Process thought does not see any line in the sand where mentality begins. Hence there is no zero-mentality at any level of the evolutionary sequence of actual entities.

There must be something more than mere matter in matter conceived as machinery, or Darwinian evolution fails to explain life. Mechanists have to explain how human beings evolved from what the mechanists call mindless matter. That is to ask how it is that humans have that attribute of mentality we call consciousness. There is no problem in attributing survival value to consciousness. To experience pain when close to a hot object enables us to withdraw to a safer place. But there are other conceivable routes to survival which do not involve consciousness. We could be zombies. These are fictitious creatures devoid of any conscious experience and yet having behaviour identical to that of their conscious counterparts. Zombies could get along all right provided they have inbuilt programmes to avoid danger and be attracted to favourable environments such as those that provide food and shelter. I know of no argument in neo-Darwinism as to why all living creatures are not zombies. Why go the route of consciousness? The mechanist has no answer. The process thinker takes another route.

The mechanist argues that mind evolved from no mind (ie, zombies). That is to invoke a miracle. But if mentality in some form were present in the building blocks of the universe we would expect there to be an evolution of mentality. And that is what seems to have happened. Zombies would be built out of a mindless universe and only a miracle would convert a zombie into a conscious being. Humans are built out of a mindful universe. That makes all the difference. The concept is that consciousness evolves from a mentality that is not conscious in atoms, to one that is conscious in higher organisms.

As one moves up levels of organisation – quarks, electrons, atoms, molecules, cells, tissues and organs – the properties of each larger whole are given not merely by the units of which it is composed but also by the new relations between these units. It is not simply that the whole is more than the sum of its parts. The parts themselves are redefined and recreated in the process of evolution from one level to another. This means that the properties of matter relevant, at say, the atomic level, do not begin to predict the properties of matter at the cellular level, let alone at the level of complex organisms.

I have drawn a contrast between an organism and a machine. The parts of a machine are subject only to the laws of mechanics. In modern machines nuts and bolts are replaced by transistors and microchips. Any change in design is bought about by the designer outside the machine. There is no evolution of machines in any real sense. This means that a completely mechanistic account of evolution is a gross abstraction from nature. It is an example of the 'fallacy of misplaced concreteness' (Whitehead 1933b p 64), of mistaking the abstract for the concrete. It was David Hume who said that the God of a mechanistic universe would be a mechanic.

Panentheism, pantheism and classical theism

As contrasted with classical theism the theism of process thought or pansubjectivism is known as panentheism; meaning 'everything is in God'. The biblical verse that describes this is found in Acts 17:28 where Paul speaks of God as one in whom 'we live and move and have our being'. Although the word 'panentheism' is literally the idea that the world, in some sense, is in God, it is also taken to include the idea that God is in some sense in the world. Panentheism differs from classical theism, which latter separates God from the world, God being conceived as occupying a supernatural sphere. It differs from pantheism which identifies God with the world. Panentheism claims that God is everywhere and permeates the world, but is not identified with it. 'God is in the world, or nowhere, creating continually in us and around us' says Whitehead (in Price 1954 p 170):

Essentially

Kabalistic

H (school

el

↓

Likute

Amarim

!!

This creative principle is everywhere in animate and so-called inanimate matter, in water, earth, human hearts. But this creation is a continuing process. And the process is itself the actuality, since no sooner do you arrive than you are on a fresh journey. In so far as man partakes of this creative process he partakes of the divine, of God ... His true destiny as cocreator of the universe is his dignity and his grandeur.

How then is the persuasive God of panentheism supposed to act in the world? I have already argued that actual entities from atoms to humans have an outer aspect (the third-person view) and an inner aspect (the first-person view). In the previous section I have argued that God acts not by determining the entities from without, but persuading them from within. God does not act on creatures as an external force. In our conscious human lives God is envisaged as whetting our appetites by confronting us with values, purposes and possibilities relevant for the moment. What then is the relationship of values to God? Whitehead proposes that God in some way contains an ordered set of values and possibilities akin to Plato's forms which Whitehead calls 'eternal objects'. This rather strange term can be replaced with one word: 'potentials'. The eternal objects are potentials of the universe. They are lures to the yet unrealised possibilities. But how do they act as causal agencies in the world? Whitehead solves this problem by naming the agency in the world the 'primordial nature of God' and naming God as an actual entity. Another way Whitehead puts this is in the proposition that possibilities of the future must reside somewhere. That somewhere, for Whitehead, is God. For materialism there is no such realm in which possibilities can exist as such. Eternal objects affect the course of events through their envisagement by God. God's influence on the whole world is analogous to the way in which mind influences the body. The primordial nature of God is thus envisaged as the ground of novelty for the universe, for it is the reservoir of all unrealised potentiality. God is not just one lure, but the infinite lure. 'God,' says Whitehead (1929 p 343) 'is not before all creation but with all creation.' This view is far removed from the God who stands outside the creation and who is imagined to directly mould each entity as a potter might mould a vase from non-reactive clay, in which God has all the creativity, the clay has none. Creation is not so much an operation from without by a supernatural being, but a process from within. It operates in terms of process and growth rather than of plan and manufacture.

Griffin (1989 p 35) points out that one of the main reasons for thinking of nature as inherently passive or uncreative is that most of the objects we touch and see, such as rocks, appear to be passive. In process thought the passive objects such as rocks are composed of multitudes of entities (atoms and molecules) that are responsive agents. It is important to think of *individual entities* that act and feel as one such as quarks. Individuals such as molecules, cells and living organisms are called compound individuals. They are more than aggregates. They are considered to have their own level of experience as individual entities. In addition there are two other categories. A rock or a star is a collection of molecules that has a certain structure but no organic unity. It is a *non-living society*. A pile of rocks is different again as there is no structural relationship between the rocks in a pile except that one rock rests on another, a pile of rocks can be called an *aggregate*. The point of this excursion is to recognise which categories of objects have an inner creative aspect. They are the actual entities such as atoms and humans. In panentheism both God and the individual entity participate in the creative process.

Two aspects of God's nature in process thought

Whitehead envisions God as having a primordial nature and a consequent nature. God's primordial nature is the presence of God in the world, God in all. It proffers the world possible values. It is eternal, and acts by persuasion. God's purpose in the world is quality of attainment. God's consequent nature is the presence of the world in God, the meaning of panentheism, all in God. God's consequent nature conserves actualised values. *It is that element that cannot be destroyed by death and gives ultimate meaning to the whole creative process.* God responds to the world with compassion. Compassion is to feel, as best one can, another's feelings. God as perfect love necessarily suffers with the world. God is not Aristotle's God of unilateral power: the 'Unmoved Mover'. The power of love, as of any relational power, is both the ability to effect and to be affected. Love that is not responsive is not love but irresponsibility.

Panentheism repudiates the doctrine of God as Unmoved Mover. In God's consequent nature God reacts to the world (is moved by the world) as it is created moment by moment. God saves the world by feeling every feeling in the world. Whatever we do makes a difference to God. What is of value in all existence is somehow saved as memory forever in the life of God. Our own feelings are added to God's ocean of feeling. Various rivers all flow together into the one ocean of feeling. It is, says Whitehead, a tender care that nothing be lost. This establishes the real importance of all we are and feel and all that the rest of creation feels. Hartshorne (1990 p 379) calls this a religion of contributionism. We contribute our feelings to others, and above all to the universal recipient of feeling, the one to whom all hearts are open. The universe would never have been as it is if we had never been! As Cobb (1993 p 192) says:

What happens is not a moment of private feeling that occurs and then is forever lost. Instead, it is forever a contribution to the divine life. God suffers with us in our suffering and rejoices with us in our joy. When we inflict pain on an animal, we inflict pain forever on God. When we ease the thirst of a neighbour, God's thirst is forever eased as well. The primary understanding of God, then, is not as lawgiver and judge but as 'the fellow sufferer who understands'.

So 'It is as true to say that *God creates the World,* as that *the World creates God*' (Whitehead 1929 p 348). The essence of Christianity, says Whitehead, is the appeal to the life of Christ as a revelation of the nature of God and of his agency in the world. Faith then is a sense of belonging to a larger reality which contributes to one's life and which receives the contribution of that life. The centrality of the person of Jesus for Christians is not that he is a God who is to control our lives but that he reveals the divine possibilities of human life. The more fully God is present in human life the more fully we are humans. The divinity that was in Jesus is the same divinity that is in us. As Harry Emerson Fosdick taught me, there are not two divinities, one for Jesus and one for us. The differences are a matter of degree, not of kind.

Name is not Jesus!

The fate of the world

The ultimate fate of 99.99 per cent of species that have ever been produced is extinction:

> 'So careful of type?' but no.
> From scarped cliff and quarried stone
> She cries, 'A thousand types are gone;
> I care for nothing. All shall go.'
>
> [**Alfred, Lord Tennyson**, 'In Memoriam', 1844]

So we return to face the fact that the ultimate fate of the world is not just the annihilation of all species, but the annihilation of every objective thing that exists, by immense heat or immense cold. Nothing will remain, not even the ruins. So what is the point or purpose of it? As I have already indicated there is none unless something survives from what looks like total annihilation. Otherwise we can only conclude with Qoheleth 'Vanity of vanities. All is vanity' (Ecclesiastes 12:8). Indeed, that is the case unless experience contributes to an abiding value that transcends annihilation of our world. Whitehead (1927 p 144) sees the passage of time as an adventure upwards and an adventure downwards:

> Whatever ceases to ascend, fails to preserve itself and enters upon its inevitable path of decay … The universe shows us two aspects: on one side it is physically wasting, on the other side it is spiritually ascending.

What then survives the perpetual perishing of every moment of every day and the ultimate annihilation of the world? There is no answer in the traditional God of classical theism. Whitehead's answer is that what is preserved eternally is the memory and experience of God in God's consequent nature. God knows the world by *feeling the feelings* of all the subjects that compose the world. The doctrine of the consequent nature of God is also known as the doctrine of objective immortality: God being the object. The world perishes but what has been achieved lives for evermore. Our existence and that of the rest of creation enriches the divine life and that is the ultimate meaning of existence. The world is saved. 'What happens really matters' says Cobb (1959 p 84) 'only if it matters ultimately, and it matters ultimately only if it matters everlastingly. What happens can matter everlastingly only if it matters to [the one] who is everlasting.'

It is now, each moment, that we miss the pearl of great price. If this vision be true then it follows that there is an aspect of God which is the same yesterday and today and forever in God's primordial nature. But there is also an aspect of God's nature that changes from day to day in God's consequent nature. God today is different from God at the time of the Big Bang. God changes. This contrasts with the notion of immutability of the God of classical theism. Soon after the Big Bang the universe provided little diversity of experience for God. Just hydrogen atoms day after day must have been a bit boring. But thereafter witnessing the creation of all the atoms and molecules, then life and dinosaurs and eventually the first humans; what an experience! The divine life was surely enriched along the route even though that route brought with it seeming waste and suffering. The purpose of God is the attainment of value in the world. God confronts what is actual in the world with what is possible for it.

Panentheism is different from classical theism in two respects:

- The primordial nature of God conceives the divine creativity as not the sole cause of creativity. Creativity is shared with the creatures.
- God's consequent nature is endlessly enriched by new experiences. God changes. What happens in the world makes a difference to God.

Why the disorders and evil in the world?

Why does disorder and evil exist in the world? There is no satisfactory answer to this question when God is claimed to be omnipotent. For how can an omnipotent loving God allow such terrible evils as the holocaust? Classical theism becomes shipwrecked on the problem of evil. This was clearly stated by

Cambridge Platonist Ralph Cudworth of the 17th century; it became known as Cudworth's dilemma. He postured: either God is neither able nor willing to eliminate evil; or God is able but not willing; or God is not able though willing; or God is both able and willing – of which only the last seems worthy of deity – and that does not happen. If God is conceived in terms of absolute power, almighty, king of kings, lord of lords, Cudworth's dilemma becomes inescapable (Raven 1953 p 121). Such an outburst is understandable. But as a theological formulation it is deficient. <u>Omnipotence is a sub-Christian concept of deity.</u> God, it is true, is spoken of in the Bible as Almighty or the Almighty. But this is an error of translation from the Hebrew (Cobb 2004 p 27). It is not the major emphasis of the Bible. Panentheism holds that it is not God alone who acts in the world. Every individual acts. Hartshorne says (1967 p 58) 'There is no single producer of the actual series of events ... what happens is in no case the product of God's creative acts alone.' In so far as the entities of creation including us have a degree of self-determination there is always the possibility of disorder and evil. God does not, cannot, overrule that freedom. If you tone down sensitivity, freedom, spontaneity and so reduce the risk of suffering, you also reduce the opportunity for depth of enjoyment. A dead person has no chance of suffering, also none of pleasure. All utopias are tame because vitality has been sacrificed to reduce risk. Every increase in the capacity for good necessarily means increase in the capacity for evil. If God had produced a world in which evil was impossible neither love nor justice nor freedom would have been possible. It would be a totalitarian state.

Really?

God's power is not one that prevents people from doing evil things. It is not magic. Instead, in God's consequent nature, God suffers with the world.

Elie Wiesel in *Night* tells of his experiences in concentration camps. He describes the death of a young boy. The following account is a paraphrase from Mesle (1993 p 76). The boy was too light in weight for the rope so that instead of dying quickly the boy lingered on gasping for breath, wriggling at the end of the rope slowly suffocating to death. One of the prisoners required to watch asked 'Where is God now?' To which another responded, 'Here he is – he is hanging there on the gallows.' Probably for that prisoner his faith in God was dying with the boy. Indeed such suffering rightly proclaims the death of faith in a God who could prevent such suffering but fails to do so. The same words can have a different meaning; God is at the end of the rope. God is sharing the suffering of the boy and also the suffering of the prisoners and the camp guards over the destruction of their humanity. God does not work magic to save us from suffering. God works in us in the struggle for justice and mercy and shares our sufferings. The existence of evil and suffering in the world of a good God has to be faced. But so too has the existence of good to be faced. There is more than the mystery of evil and suffering to be explained. There is the mystery of good. It is a mystery that out of the Big Bang with its incredible high temperatures and explosions that a world emerges in which values and goodness are survivors. Had we been observers of the Big Bang how could we even dream that it was to lead to a world of values and goodness?

The concept of the consequent nature of God is that God experiences all experiences. It is a view that can neither be proved or disproved. It is a necessary completion of the idea of God if the whole argument is to make sense and contributes to elucidation so that we see things in a new light that were previously shrouded in darkness. Furthermore, framing a concept of God is not just an intellectual exercise. It affects our lives. As we think so we live. As our faith is so will our character be. More speculative, it seems to me, than objective immortality is the concept of subjective immortality, the survival of the subject in some form of individual life after death. Whitehead emphasises objective immortality, nevertheless he leaves the door open for interpretations of subjective immortality.

How much does God know?

In much of classical theism God is supposed to know not only the past and the present but the future as well. It is as though time is a picture of the world's history spread out as fully settled. If that is the case there is no freedom. All is pre-determined. This view has been invoked as the doctrine of omniscience along with the doctrine of omnipotence of God. Process theism rejects both. Instead of the omniscience of God process theism promotes a concept of God as knowing the past in memory and the present as present experience and the future as a range of possibilities not yet determined in the world. These ideas about God are developed in *The Liberation of Life* by Birch and Cobb (1981), *Feelings* by Birch (1995), and *Biology and the Riddle of Life* by Birch (1999).

God in the world and the world in God

In summary we can think of the God of compassion as involving three principles: the presence of God in the world; the responsiveness of the world to God; and the presence of the world in God.

'Thou art all compassion, pure unbounded love thou art' is how Charles Wesley's hymn puts the presence of God in the world. In every event we are addressed by God's compassionate love as is the whole of creation. God's activity is not intermittent. God is never off duty as a compassionate influence. The world lives by the incarnation of God in itself. If God were withdrawn for a moment the creation would no longer exist. God is the lure of the world and acts exclusively by persuasion, never by coercion. Is God then powerless? The paradox of power is that in the end the only power that matters is the power of persuasive love.

The responsiveness of the world to God is by God being felt by his creatures. God confronts what is actual in the world with what is possible for it at that moment. A note from a tuning fork elicits a response from the piano because the piano already has a string tuned to that same note. We, and the creation, are similarly attuned to the influence of God. For humans the only adequate response to God's love is infinite passion; with all of one's heart and mind and strength. The whole of creation is waiting for its liberation from its bondage under human exploitation.

The presence of the world in God is expressed by George Matheson, afflicted by blindness, when he wrote:

O love that will not let me go,
I rest my weary soul in Thee,
I give Thee back the life I owe,
That in Thine ocean depths its flow
May richer, fuller be.

The last three lines express the author's feeling that his life contributed to the ocean of God's life of feeling. Real love has a twofold aspect. On the one hand is the love that gives. On the other hand is the love that receives. Love that leaves the lover unaffected by the joys and sufferings of the one who is loved is not worthy of being called love at all. God experiences the world as it is created in both its joys and agonies. According to Jesus not a sparrow falls to the ground without God knowing. God is not a counter of dead sparrows but the suggestion is they count in God's life.

There are three principles of the universe in the vision of process theology:

1. In every event we and the creation are addressed by God's compassion.
2. In every event we are called to express God's compassion for us and the creation.
3. In every event, what we do and what the creation does make a difference to God.

In this vision the divine is not the supreme autocrat but the universal agent of persuasion, whose power is the worship it inspires, and who feels all the feelings of the world. I find this not only a new way of understanding the world, but also a new way of facing the tasks of today in the human crisis and the environmental crisis.

What then is the promise? It is not that everything will come to a good end? Many things come to a bad end. It is the faith that nothing can prevent us from fulfilling the ultimate meaning of our existence, neither holocaust, nor poverty, neither principalities nor powers, neither dictators nor tyrants. No matter how great the evil in the world God acts persuasively to bestow whatever good is still possible. This is borne out by some of the survivors of concentration camps who managed to find some hope in the midst of their despair in the visit of a bird to their window sill, the sight of a tree in the distance, a sunset or the thought of a beloved spouse, all of which inspired the possibility of eventual freedom. The victim could not change the circumstances but could change one's attitude toward them. While life exists there is hope. Those who had even a skerrick of hope had a greater chance of surviving the ordeal of the concentration camp.

This then is the promise: a sense of belonging to a larger reality which contributes to one's life and the life of all creatures and which receives the contribution of that life.

Those who are unfamiliar with the concept of God in panentheism and who come from a conservative or a fundamentalist tradition ask two questions: 'Is the God of panentheism personal?' and 'Can that God be worshiped?' If I were to give a yes or no answer I would say yes the God of this tradition is personal. But there are many problems with the word 'personal'. This word is bound up with a substance way of thinking. We tend to think of persons as separate entities like chairs and tables. Persons are not like that. A person is what he or she is by virtue of their internal relations. They are not like substances. Part of the problem is the way Christian theologians in the 4th century introduced the doctrine of the trinity to embrace the supposed three persons of the Godhead which easily became a tritheism or three substances. In the 3rd century Tertullian, who invented the dogma of the trinity, used the Greek word *persona*. It means the mask of an actor through which a special character is portrayed. So trinity speaks of three aspects of the divine. Better say God is not a person but God is personal. Indeed the relations Christians claim to experience with God are highly personal and transformative of life.

Can one worship such a God? The word 'worship' means 'ascription of worth to'. I ascribe worth wherever I find intrinsic value especially in humans. But I don't worship humans as such but the source of their intrinsic value that is God. This is the distinction we made earlier between created goods and creative good. Wieman (1929) considers there are three conditions which must be met before effective worship is possible: seriousness, sincerity and seclusion from distractions. Seriousness is contrasted with a life of trivialities. Sincerity is being honest with oneself about what one regards as of ultimate concern. Seclusion is freedom from distractions. Perhaps the latter condition is what Whitehead (1927 p 6) meant when he said 'religion is what an individual does with his own solitariness'. He went on to say that if you are never solitary you are not religious. Solitariness is not solitude but the opposite. When I am alone I am not alone.

History of pansubjectivism and panentheism

The contemporary inspiration of constructive postmodernism or pansubjectivism and panentheism is chiefly the 20th century philosopher and mathematician AN Whitehead. Other contemporary exponents include Charles Hartshorne, John Cobb, David Griffin, Marjorie Suchocki and Schubert Ogden. Yet, in a less developed form, pansubjectivity has had a noble tradition in philosophy (Skrbina 2003) from the earliest writings of the pre-Socratic thinkers such as Thales, coming to the fore again in some of the writings of Plato (eg, *anima mundi* or 'world soul') and Aristotle. Five of the most important 16th century philosophers of the Italian Renaissance – Gerolamo Cardano, Bernardino Telesio, Francesco Patrizi, Giordano Bruno and Tommaso Campanella – were pansubjectivists. Benedictus de Spinoza and Gottfried Leibniz of the 17th century were pansubjectivists. In the 18th century several major German philosophers had pansubjectivist views, they include Arthur Schopenhauer, Johann Wolfgang von Goethe, and Ernst Haeckel (Skrbina 2003). In the 19th and 20th century Hartshorne and Reese (1953) consider the following were panentheists and by implication pansubjectivists or close to it: Friedrich Schelling, Gustav Fechner, Otto Pfleiderer, Bernardino Varisco, AN Whitehead, Nikolai Berdyaev, Muhammad Iqbal, Albert Schweitzer, Martin Buber, Sarvepalli Radhakrishnan,

Paul Weiss, and Alan Watts. Griffin et al (1993) consider that the founders of constructive postmodern philosophy in the 19th and 20th centuries were CS Peirce, William James, Henri Bergson, AN Whitehead and Charles Hartshorne. Today the tradition is promoted in a number of centres of process studies around the world, but particularly in the Center for Process Studies in Claremont California where John Cobb and David Griffin, among others, have been guiding lights.

Panentheism in an ancient form goes back to Pharaoh Ikhnaton (1375–58 BC), who was the first monotheist. It also can be found in Hindu and Judeo–Christian scriptures.

Practical consequences

A distinction can be made between inner commitment and outer commitment. One concerns values to which we have committed ourselves. The other concerns the extent to which we translate those values into effective action. Belief is an inner commitment on which one is prepared to act. When someone says his belief is that life has no meaning and no value, yet goes on living, he can be challenged to prove what he means by what he says he believes. When I put this proposition to a clever friend of mine who says there is no ultimate purpose in the world he replied that when the proposition confronts him he goes into his bedroom, pulls down the blinds, lies on the bed and tries to forget its implications.

Of any proposition it is well to relate belief to action by asking the question: 'What use is it?' It is asked of the work of the astronomer, the evolutionary biologist, the philosopher, the theologian and those of other disciplines. I had a friend who was an astronomer. He not only looked at stars but designed a telescope called an interferometer. The telescope happened to be on the route of a tourist bus in Narrabri in New South Wales. The tourists got out of their bus and had a look at the telescope and listened to the astronomer give a brief talk. The one sure question from the tourists was: 'What use is it?' The astronomer later wrote a book about the use of science that he called *The Wisdom of Science* (Hanbury Brown 1986). He argued that the most valuable 'use' of science was the getting of wisdom. He had been somewhat miffed by the attitude of non-scientists on a committee of which he was a member giving advice to the Australian government. Some of the non-scientists thought that science was, like ballet dancing, a cultural asset. Instead he argued that science had been responsible for the demise of superstition and the basing of community welfare on facts resulting in the creation of the modern world. Science had changed our world with its ideas and commitments.

That could also be the 'use' of universities? If you walk from *Unter den Linden* to the main entrance hall of Humboldt University in Berlin, as I did recently, you will see a central wall of marble taken from Adolf Hitler's demolished chancellery. It represents a past. But on that same wall in large gold letters are these words by Karl Marx: 'The philosophers have only interpreted the world in various ways, the real task is to *change* it.' The philosopher AN Whitehead had a similar idea when he said the mission of the university is the creation of the future. That is its use.

On his 100th birthday Charles Hartshorne was interviewed by a journalist of the *US News*. The interview was published under the headline 'A hundred years of thinking about God.' The journalist may have had the question 'What use is it?' in the back of his mind. Hartshorne said that we live in a century in which everything seems to have been said. There are propositions about the meaning of life and the meaning of God in a scientific world.

The challenge today, he said, is to learn which statements to deny if we are to discover the truth by which to live. Our confusion is not due to our having too little information, but too much. Implicit in Hartshorne's statement is that out of this last century of thought we need to decipher the truth. The use of that is it leads us to how we are to live. We need a focus to live by and a vision of the good life and the good society. Ultimately what matters is that our inner commitment leads to an outer commitment. Consider Jesus. Despite the fact that his family called him 'beside himself' and that his church called him a heretic, that his nation's rulers regarded him as a public menace to be liquidated, that he was betrayed by his friend and crucified by his government, Jesus never said: 'I have explained the world.' He did say: 'I have overcome the world.'

Whatever understanding we have of the world is only a tiny part of the world, leaving the rest to await further enlightenment or perhaps forever to remain a mystery. It is important that the tiny part we do understand should be an inner commitment that leads to outer commitment that will help transform our life and that of the world around us.

In the modern world we are faced with a problem of the amount of knowledge that accumulates at such a great rate. This leads to increased professionalism or specialisation. Yet the world right now has problems that spread over many specialities as is indicated below. Specialisation leads in the opposite direction. It produces minds in a groove. The modern university illustrates this with its many departments, from arts to zoology, whose staff hardly talk to one another. The call for inter-department programmes leaves the basic causes of the problem unresolved. The problem is the division of knowledge with its artificial boundaries. The philosopher VW Quine said that boundaries are made for deans and librarians.

Daly and Cobb (1989 Chapter 6) make some radical proposals stimulated by process thought, for dethroning what they call disciplinolatry in universities. This book leads us to re-evaluate many areas of life such as our environment, energy use, justice, science and technology, peace and equality of the sexes. I was involved for 20 years in a working group of the World Council of Churches committed to what it called the Just Participatory and Sustainable Society. My judgments about this programme have been made in light of my own understanding of the meaning of life. Others in the group had a more traditional view of things. Together we wanted to work out the implications of our programme for the wellbeing of the world. Much has been published on our deliberations. I mention just four books that are in part particularly oriented to a process understanding: *The Liberation of Life* (Birch and Cobb 1981), *Genetics and the Quality of Life* (Birch and Abrecht 1975), *Liberating Life* (Birch, Eakin and McDaniel 1994) and *Living with the Animals* (Birch and Vischer 1997).

In what follows I shall give a brief account of that aspect of the programme that deals with two values: an instrumental value namely the ecologically sustainable society and the intrinsic value of living creatures. Our prime concern should be the enhancement of the richness of experience of individual human beings and the living organisms that share and feel the Earth with us. To be sustainable is to be capable of indefinite existence. Yet the present world community is committed to continuous economic growth, which cannot continue forever. There are limits to growth in use of resources and deterioration of environment that goes along with growth. In essence, the sustainable society is one with a stable population and a fixed material wealth per person. It is also active in pursuing quality of life in such things as leisure, services and sport. The phrase 'ecological sustainability', which originated in this programme of the World Council of Churches, emphasised the necessity of sustaining the life-support systems of the Earth and the resources on which they depend. It is an ecological sustainability. But it has a wider context as well: the sustainability of the structures of social and political systems. It could be argued that no country as yet has a sustainable political system that ensures increased wellbeing of all human beings. We can learn from ecologically sustainable natural communities of plants and animals such as in a rainforest. It is little appreciated that a natural community such as a rainforest recycles all materials used as resources. Apart from water and carbon dioxide the only resource that comes from outside is the energy of the sun. It is a ready-made model for us to learn from.

The world is far from being ecologically sustainable. With so much injustice and oppression it is easy to understand why many people have focussed on these two problems, by-passing the issue of sustainability. Their ethic has been anthropocentric. It was somewhat of a triumph for some of us when the World Council of Churches (WCC) agreed to sponsor, at our suggestion, a symposium on the wellbeing of living organisms that share the Earth with us (see further Chapter 4). They too are oppressed, even to the point of extinction. Our report (see Birch, Eakin and McDaniel 1994) was widely distributed to animal liberation groups, especially in the US, largely due to the activity of one member of the consultation. As a result of this publicity the general secretary of the WCC received many hostile communications from hunting groups, furriers and the like. Our report produced more response from secular organisations than any for a long time. Before the consultation I had asked the general secretary of the WCC if he would take any notice of our efforts. He replied 'not unless you can show that it will help the starving people in Bangladesh'. We have a long way to go! Besides suffering people in Bangladesh, non-human animals too are a part of the suffering life on Earth. Because each individual animal has feelings it too has rights that should result in its wellbeing. Hence, for example, 'Project Tiger' in India, aims to take care of such tigers as remain in that country.

The rights of animals have long been a concern of people who were also humanitarian reformers; among them Voltaire, Jeremy Bentham, John Stuart Mill, Bernard Shaw and, in our own time, Peter Singer. They have been at the forefront of campaigners for the rights of non-human animals as well as human beings. These concerns lead some people to refuse to eat animals or use them for clothing. Others concentrate on improving the lot of farm animals and those native animals whose habitats are threatened by the spread of human communities. Further concerns have to do with experimentation on animals, ownership of patents for genetically engineered organisms, and also the use of animals for entertainment, such as bull-fighting. The Humane Society in the US lists many additional concerns. We are called on to act with respect and concern for animals. This is not just an act of mercy but of justice as well. The practical task of a biocentric ethic as contrasted with an anthropocentric ethic is to rightly balance the intrinsic value of each creature with its instrumental worth. This means taking into account an elephant's right to live and its negative instrumental value to the land-owner whose space and crops it might ravage. The task is daunting, but remember the words of Margaret Mead, 'never doubt what a small group of thoughtful citizens can do to change the world. Indeed, it is the only thing that ever has.'

In the vision of God who is not the supreme autocrat but the universal agent of persuasion, who feels all the feelings of the world, I find not only a new way of understanding the world, but also a new way of facing the tasks of today in recognition of the human and environmental crisis. Committed people want to know what they can do. A successful career woman had enough of making money and wanted to give something back. She asked 'how?' In her puzzlement she wrote to Mother Teresa in Calcutta, offered to volunteer and sought her advice. A one-sentence reply came from Mother Teresa 'Thank you for your offer, but find your own Calcutta.'

From what I have written it is obvious that some of my mentors have had more influence than others in shaping my view of life. I learned science and the social responsibility of scientists primarily from Andrewartha and Dobzhansky. Some of them such as Agar, Waddington and Sewall Wright reinforced my philosophy of life as it was shaped by process thought. We shared the same understanding. My philosophical understanding of religion came mainly from Fosdick, Hartshorne, Tillich and Niebuhr. Behind it all was the influence of Whitehead and his modern interpreters, Hartshorne, Cobb and Griffin and their school of process thought in Claremont, California. They keep the door open for yet further understandings. What we know is a mere drop in the ocean and an infinity of further novel experiences await us. I recall Hartshorne saying that a thousand year programme of research lay ahead of us in process thought. And as Whitehead (1938 pp 168–9) said:

Philosophy begins in wonder. And at the end, when philosophic thought has done its best, the wonder remains. There have been added, however, some grasp of the immensity of things, some purification of emotion by understanding.

REFERENCES

Agar, WE (1943) *A Contribution to the Theory of the Living Organism*. Melbourne: Melbourne University Press.

Allee, WC, Emerson, A, Park, O, Park, T and Schmidt, K (1949) *Principles of Animal Ecology*. Philadelphia: WB Saunders Co.

Andrewartha, HG and Birch, LC (1954) *The Distribution and the Abundance of Animals*. Chicago: University of Chicago Press.

Andrewartha, HG and Birch, LC (1984) *The Ecological Web*. Chicago: University of Chicago Press.

Anon (1954) *Contemporary Civilization in the West*. Vol 1. New York: Columbia University Press.

Baillie, J (1951) *Natural Science and the Spiritual Life*. Oxford: Oxford University Press.

Barbour, IG (1990) *Religion in an Age of Science*. London: SCM Press.

Bergson, H (1911) *Creative Evolution*. New York: Henry Holt and Company.

Birch, LC (1990) *On Purpose*. Sydney: UNSW Press.

Birch, LC (1993) *Regaining Compassion: For humanity and nature*. Sydney: UNSW Press.

Birch, LC (1995) *Feelings*. Sydney: UNSW Press.

Birch, LC (1999) *Biology and the Riddle of Life*. Sydney: UNSW Press.

Birch, LC and Abrecht, P (eds) (1975) *Genetics and the Quality of Life*. Sydney: Pergamon Press.

Birch, LC and Cobb, JB (1981) *The Liberation of Life*. Cambridge: Cambridge University Press. Reprinted by Environmental Ethics Books.

Birch, LC, Eakin, W and McDaniel, JB (eds) (1994) *Liberating Life*. Maryknoll: Orbis Books.

Birch, LC and Vischer, L (1997) *Living with the Animals*. Geneva: World Council of Churches Publications.

Borg, M (1987) *Jesus: A new vision*. San Francisco: HarperCollins.

Borg, M (1995) *Meeting Jesus Again for the First Time*. San Francisco: HarperCollins.

Brown, D, James, RE and Reeves, G (1971) *Process Philosophy and Christian Thought*. New York: Bobbs-Merrill.

Chesterton, GK (1934) *St Francis of Assisi*. London: Hodder and Stoughton.

Cobb, JB (1959) *God and the World*. Philadelphia: Westminster Press.

Cobb, JB (1991) *Can Christ Become Good News Again?* St Louis: Chalice Press.

Cobb, JB (1993) 'AN Whitehead' in DR Griffin, JB Cobb, MP Ford, PAY Gunter, P Ochs (eds) *Founders of Constructive Postmodern Philosophy*. Albany: State University of New York Press, pp 165–95.

Cobb, JB (2004) *Process Theology: An introductory introduction*. Claremont: Process and Faith Press.

Daly, HE and Cobb, JB (1989) *For the Common Good*. Boston: Beacon Press.

Dawkins, R (2006) *The God Delusion*. London: Bantam Press.

Dobzhansky, T (1937) *Genetics and the Origin of Species*. New York: Columbia University Press.

Ferre, F (2001) *Living and Value: Towards a constructive postmodern ethics*. Albany: State University of New York Press.

Feynman, RP (1998) *The Meaning of It All*. London: Penguin.

Fosdick, HE (1961) *The Greatness of God*. London: Collins.

Fox, W (2006) *A Theory of General Ethics*. Cambridge: MIT Press.

Frankl, V (1969) 'Reductionism and nihilism' in A Koestler and JR Smythies (eds) *Beyond Reductionism*. London: Hutchinson, pp 369–408.

Frankl, V (1959) *Man's Search for Meaning*. London: Hodder and Stoughton.

Franklin, J (2003) *Corrupting the Youth: A history of philosophy in Australia*. Sydney: Macleay Press.

Gardner, M (1973) *The Flight of Peter Fromm*. Los Altos: William Kaufmann.

Gardner, M (1997) *The Night at Large*. London: Penguin.

Griffin, DR (1989) *God and Religion in the Postmodern World*. Albany: State University of New York Press.

Griffin, DR (1998) *Unsnarling the World-Knot: Consciousness, freedom, and the mind-body problem*. Berkeley: University of California Press.

Griffin, DR (2000) *Religion and Scientific Naturalism: Overcoming the conflicts*. Albany: State University of New York Press.

Griffin, DR, Cobb, JB, Ford, MP, Gunter, PAY and Ochs, P (eds) (1993) *Founders of Constructive Postmodern Philosophy*. Albany: State University of New York Press.

Hanbury Brown, R (1986) *The Wisdom of Science*. Cambridge: Cambridge University Press.

Hartshorne, C (1953) *Reality as Social Process*. Glencoe: The Free Press.

Hartshorne, C (1962) *The Logic of Perfection*. La Salle: Open Court.

Hartshorne, C (1967) *A Natural Theology for our Time*. La Salle: Open Court.

Hartshorne, C (1971) 'The development of process philosophy' in EH Cousins (ed) *Process Theology*. New York: Newman Press, pp 47–66.

Hartshorne, C (1990) *The Darkness and the Light*. Albany: State University of New York Press.

Hartshorne, C (1997) *The Zero Fallacy and Other Essays in Neoclassical Philosophy*. La Salle: Open Court.

Hartshorne, C and Reese, WL (1953) *Philosophers Speak of God*. Chicago: University of Chicago Press.

Henning, BG (2005) *The Ethics of Creativity: Beauty, morality and nature in a processive cosmos*. Pittsburgh: University of Pittsburgh Press.

Hutchins, RM (1946) *Education for Freedom*. Baton Rouge: Louisiana University Press.

Huxley, J (1942) *Evolution: The modern synthesis*. New York: Harper & Brothers.

Keller, C and Daniell, A (2002) *Process and Difference: Between cosmological and poststructuralist postmodernisms*. Albany: State University of New York Press.

Keynes, John Maynard (1936) *The General Theory of Employment, Interest and Money*. Cambridge: Cambridge University Press.

Lewontin, RC (1981) 'The scientific work of Th. Dobzhansky' in RC Lewontin, JA Moore, WB Provine and B Wallace (eds) *Dobzhansky's Genetics of Natural Populations*. New York: Columbia University Press, pp 93–115.

Livingstone, RW (1946) *The Greek Genius and its Meaning to Us*. Oxford: Oxford University Press.

MacIntyre, A (1981) *After Virtue: A study in moral theory*. London: Duckworth.

May, R (1988) *Paulus: Tillich as spiritual teacher*. Dallas: Saybrook.

Mayr, E (1942) *Systematics and the Origin of Species*. New York: Columbia University Press.

Mesle, CR (1993) *Process Theology: A basic introduction*. St Louis: Chalice Press.

McNeill, WH (1991) *Hutchins' University: A memoir of the University of Chicago 1929–1950*. Chicago: University of Chicago Press.

Pearson, K (1899) *The Grammar of Science*. London: Macmillan.

Price, L (1954) *Dialogues with Alfred North Whitehead*. Boston: Little Brown and Company.

Randers, J, Meadows, HD, Meadows, DL, Behrens, W (1972) *The Limits to Growth*. New York: New American Library.

Raven, CE (1953) *Natural Religion and Christian Theology*. Cambridge: Cambridge University Press.

Russell, B (1956) *Portraits from Memory*. London: Allen and Unwin.

Russell, B (1968) *The Impact of Science on Society*. London: Allen and Unwin.

Simpson, GG (1944) *Tempo and Mode in Evolution*. New York: Columbia University Press.

Singer, P (1993) *How Are We to Live?* Melbourne: Text Publishing.

Skrbina, D (2003) 'Panpsychism as an underlying theme in Western philosophy'. *Journal of Consciousness Studies*. 10 (3), pp 4–46.

Sokal, A and Bricmont, J (1998) *Intellectual Postures*. London: Profile. Published in the US by Picador as *Fashionable Nonsense*.

Stebbins, L (1950) *Variation and Evolution in Plants*. New York: Columbia University Press.

Stove, D (2003) 'Why have philosophers?' in J Franklin, *Corrupting the Youth: A history of philosophy in Australia*. Sydney: Macleay Press, pp 431–3.

Tarnas, R (1991) *The Passion of the Western Mind*. New York: Ballantine.

Teilhard de Chardin, P (1955) *The Phenomenon of Man*. New York: Harper & Row.

Thorpe, WH (1958) *Learning and Instinct in Animals*. Cambridge: Harvard University Press.

Tillich, P (1948) *The Protestant Era*. Chicago: University of Chicago Press.

Tillich, P (1963) *The Eternal Now*. London: SCM Press.

Tillich, P (1967) *A History of Christian Thought*. New York: Simon and Schuster.

Waddington, CH (1963) *The Nature of Life*. London: Allen and Unwin.

Wester, D (1948) 'Can metaphysics save the world?' *Saturday Review of Literature*. 10 April. 1948, pp 7–8.

Whitehead, AN (1927) *Religion in the Making*. Cambridge: Cambridge University Press.

Whitehead, AN (1929) *Process and Reality*. DR Griffin and D Sherboune (eds) (revised ed 1978) New York: Free Press.

Whitehead, AN (1933a) *Adventure of Ideas*. New York: Free Press.

Whitehead, AN (1933b) *Science and the Modern World*. Cambridge: Cambridge University Press.

Whitehead, AN (1938) *Modes of Thought*. New York: Free Press.

Whitehead, AN (1966) *The Function of Reason*. Boston: Beacon Press.

Wieman, HN (1929) *Methods of Private Religious Living*. New York: Macmillan.

Wieman, HN (1946) *The Source of Human Good*. Chicago: University of Chicago Press.

Wilson, AN (1988) *Tolstoy*. London: Hamish Hamilton.

INDEX